WISDOM , INSIGHTS,
& ADVICE FROM A
LIFETIME ON
WALL STREET

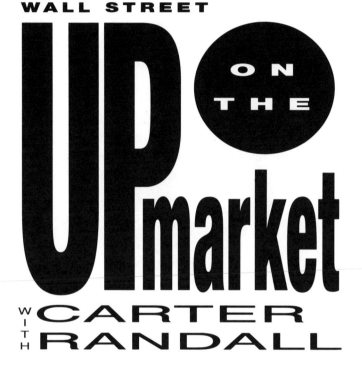

UP ON THE market

WITH CARTER RANDALL

AS TOLD TO
WILLIAM J. GIANOPULOS

PROBUS PUBLISHING COMPANY
Chicago, Illinois
Cambridge, England

Cover photo: Beverly Brosius Photographer, Winter Park, FL
Graphs courtesy of Mr. Hani N. Tawil

ISBN 1-55738-263-8

Printed in the United States of America

BB

1 2 3 4 5 6 7 8 9 0

contents

preface

I take a great deal of pride in my work. Admittedly, some readers might find this rather puzzling. After all, I have spent most of my adult life as a conservative, pinstripe-suited banker and, like many of this sort, I have walked around with a big, black, ominous cloud over my head, thinking deep, dark thoughts as I have managed investment funds for others.

But, I am fortunate because I have also been engaged in other diverse activities, which have propelled me in directions I could never have imagined when I started in the business. In addition to appearing for twenty years on national television, I have written articles for newspapers and magazines, taught various college courses, and traveled the nation speaking before audiences of varied backgrounds, ages, and interests. I am understandably proud of those extra-curricular activities, but not for the reasons one might suspect.

The source of my pride is that I am helping to educate people about the economic system under which they live. It is my general observation that the American people are very poorly educated about economics and, in particular, about the capitalistic system. Yet, they live under such a system, and it makes sense that if they fail to understand it they will have some difficulty with it.

Even worse, the fact that people do not understand something makes it all the more difficult for them to support it. And if the American people do not well understand the capitalistic system, we run the risk of losing it.

I could debate both sides of whether or not capitalism is the best economic system devised by man, but the argument itself makes little difference. Capitalism remains the order under which we live, and if we lose it because of lack of understanding and support, there will be chaos in this nation not for weeks, months or years but, literally, for generations to come.

If I can participate in helping people understand and support—as well as improve—our capitalistic system, then I feel I am contributing something to both myself and others; hence my pride.

If this book helps people make wise decisions about how to invest their money in the securities markets of our capitalistic system, then I will consider my efforts worthwhile.

Carter Randall

acknowledgements

A book is not the creation of just one person. It requires many. My profound thanks go to those who encouraged me to put this book together. Without my friends at Probus, there would have been little encouragement to forge ahead with this project. Without my co-author, Bill Gianopulos, there would have been no book. As a matter of fact, although the thoughts are mine, many of the words are his.

And then, of course, I dedicate this book, as I dedicate almost everything, to my wife, Nancy; to my children, Cathy and Carroll; to Nancy's children, Mike, Greg, Beverly, and David; and to their spouses, Winston, Charlie, Cookie, Emilie, Kevin, and Katherine. And I hope those little ones, who will be important people of the 21st century—Ian, Emma, Rick, Alix, Savannah, and Dan, not to mention the yet unnamed little ones about to be—will remember their grandfather.

I owe each and every one of these people my appreciation for who they are, what they have done, and what they will be. Without all of them, there is nothing.

prologue

prologue

"wall street week
with louis rukeyser"

In the spring of 1970, I received a call from Anne Darlington, a producer at the Maryland Center for Public Broadcasting, who informed me that she was working on a new television program called "Wall Street Week," which she hoped to produce. The program idea was apparently in response to a need for more public information concerning both the investment markets and the economy. She invited me to audition as a possible participant in the program and, of course, I was interested and intrigued.

That, for me, was the beginning of a new way of life. I had performed some public speaking, had been involved in money management for over twenty years, was a Vice President of a bank and trust company, but had never appeared before a television camera.

In addition to me, dozens of others also auditioned. We were asked to read a script on a teleprompter, to give "top of the head" commentaries, and to answer questions concerning our backgrounds and areas of expertise. Virtually all of those who auditioned were members of the Baltimore financial community. At that time, the program was to be produced locally with the hope that it would be broadcast at least regionally and, in time, nationally.

I was never privy to all of the machinations that went into the selection of the cast of characters who participated, but I do know that a group of us was selected for varying reasons.

First, of course, we had to demonstrate some expertise in the subject matter. But I also recall that there were many other reasons for selection. Chief among them (though not necessarily ranked in order of importance) were our looks, our diversity of occupations and backgrounds, and our speaking ability. The most important criterion, as I recall, was our ability to say something of substance in a relatively short period of time. The prudent use of time is important to every successful television program because, of course, time is limited.

One decision that was made about the program, which was vital to its eventual success, was choosing a competent and stimulating moderator. With few exceptions, none of those interviewed or auditioned had proven experience in the broadcast media or, for that matter, in economic journalism. And so, from the very start, it was apparent that the program needed a professional in this field to emcee or host the program. There could not have been a better choice for this than Louis Rukeyser. Not only did he have experience in all forms of journalism, but he had a solid background in economics. Of course, he also had good looks and intriguing mannerisms, a quick, intelligent mind, a superb speaking voice, a great sense of humor, and many other attributes to qualify him for the role.

In any case, several of us survived the ordeal of the audition, and the plan was for us to appear on a rotating basis so that different, new, and even disparate views would be aired. All of those chosen (I like to think this is true of me too) were professional investment advisors with areas of expertise in various areas of money management, economics, security analysis, etc. Represented were practicing members of the brokerage, investment counseling, trust, and mutual funds industries.

I think it is fair to say that at that time Frank Cappiello and I were considered the "prime panelists." At least in the early weeks of the show, we appeared each week along with other panelists who rotated. It may or may not be that we were considered "good," but we were available, and continuity of the cast of characters was considered important.

The very first program was aired to a regional audience on November 20, 1970. I remember it well. Our adrenalin level was high and we were quite excited about our debut, almost the way a child would feel before a school play. The format of the show was essentially the same as it is today: opening remarks by Lou Rukeyser, followed by a panel discussion about the economy and the state of the investment markets, and an interview of a special guest. The special guest that night was Stan West of the New York Stock Exchange, who discussed in detail the make up of the demographics of investors.

The rest is history. Some things have changed, while others have remained the same. Added to the format of the program was a segment devoted to answering viewer questions. The physical setting has been altered a few times, but the basic format has remained consistent with the original.

That is not to say that there have not been some more substantive changes. Indeed, there have been several. Foremost among them is that the program soon aired nationally.

There have been some remote location broadcasts, and there have been many special broadcasts.

The participation and mix of panelists and guests has also changed. Whereas all of the original panelists were from the Baltimore area, now they are from various places—Baltimore, New York (most of them), Chicago, San Francisco, etc. Wherever we live and work (I have lived in Florida since 1977), we commute to Owings Mill, Maryland, to do the broadcast. There are currently a total of twenty-eight panelists, most of whom have been featured guests in the past, representing a broad spectrum of professions, from money managers to specialists in fields of investment, including market letter writers, analysts, fundamental researchers, technical market experts, bond specialists, and on and on the list goes.

We do not always agree with each other; in fact, it is a rare occasion when all three panelists on any show agree on such matters as the economic outlook, predictions for the investment markets, and advice offered to investors. This may be confusing to some of our viewers, but I strongly believe that it is important that disparate views be aired because, in the real investment world, it is ever thus. Rarely are such subjects cast in bronze or the issues self-evident. I think the disparity in views is a vital component to an interesting and informative program.

I have a great deal of respect for my fellow panelists. Though I may agree or disagree with them, I recognize their expertise, knowledge, and experience. They are all consummate professionals. And we have a common bond. We are all proud of being participants in the program, and we are all not only dedicated to its success but also determined to offer information and assistance to help investors make sound decisions about what to do with their money. This is an unwritten but vital creed of "Wall Street Week with Louis Rukeyser."

Do I have any reservations about my participation on the program? Of course. First and foremost, I regret that my comments or advice have not always been on the mark. And, unfortunately, even when I know by hindsight that I have been wrong, rarely is there a chance to correct what I have said. And, of course, time constraints do not allow us to say everything we think about a given subject nor even discuss all of the pros and cons of our positions.

To be asked a question about a relatively complicated subject and to answer the question in thirty or forty seconds does an injustice to the subject. But this is one of the problems of the broadcast media in general; often, the viewer or listener sees or hears only the "tip of the iceberg," not the full story. Very often, people remind me of what I did not say or what I should have explained, and most of the time I agree with them, but such is the way of life in television. My hope is that most of the time my comments will stimulate the thinking of viewers.

I am prone to say what I think at the time I say it, and I believe that most viewers recognize this as a limitation. To those who thank me for the good advice I give or to those who criticize me for what I say, I offer the same response: accept what I say as what I think, but know that I am fallible and that circumstances can occur which will either bolster or negate what I say. No one, in my opinion, should take precipitous action on money management or investment selection based on a thirty-second opinion aired on television, even if he has total confidence in the person who recommends such action.

There are many questions people ask about the program but there are several which they ask repeatedly.

For example, people ask what kind of fellow Louis Rukeyser really is. My answer is that he is really what the viewer sees and hears. He is very intelligent, quick-witted, and able. People often want to know whether or not Lou writes his "own stuff." And, of course, his answer and mine is, he does. Lou has help in compiling facts and figures and is quite willing to hear suggestions, but what he says is his "own stuff." And he does a superb job. Not only does he have a great grasp of what is happening in the social, political, economic, and investment market worlds, he has a unique ability to convey it concisely and in his own inimitable style.

To those who may criticize his humor (most people love it), I suggest that it is the catalyst which ignites the attention of the viewer, and without that style, the audience would be much smaller than it is. Even I will admit that economics and investments could be dry, dull, technical, and boring subjects without some humor thrown in.

And there is another kudo I would throw to Lou. He is a superb interviewer. Not only does he ask intelligent questions (questions the answers to which viewers want), but he listens to the answers and reacts to them. This is not necessarily a skill which all interviewers exhibit; many will ask questions but care little about the answers. Lou's ability to react to statements, challenge them, dig deeper, "play the devil's advocate," correct mistakes, and ask for explanations is without peer. And Lou's desire to bring the high science of economics down to earth is certainly evident each time he asks a panelist or a special guest to simplify his technical, unfamiliar, or confusing language. Lou acts as an advocate of the viewer, and this is not just a valuable service but a rare ability.

Many people ask "who are the elves?" They are referring, of course, to Louis Rukeyser's references to the so-called "elves" who do mysterious things! The "elves of the black forest" are a select group of technical market analysts who inform the program weekly whether or not they are "bullish," "bearish," or "neutral" on the direction of the market for the next six months. The Wall Street Week Technical Market Index is strictly a compilation of how many are positive, how many neutral, and how many negative. There are ten such analysts (I am not one of them), and they are among the most followed analysts in Wall Street. Whether their numerical opinions can consistently predict the future of the market or whether, in fact, the index can be used as a "contrary indicator" has been and will always be debated. But, at least, viewers are made aware of what these experts are thinking.

Another question often asked is "who is that girl?" Reference is made to the omnipresent lady who acts as a hostess on the program but who never participates in the discussion. She is a very important part of the program. Although her role appears to be superfluous, she fills a need. First of all, she not only accompanies the special guest to the set to make sure he or she appears at the right place at the right time, but she performs other functions. Her role is a throwback to early television when programs were almost always live (and a good portion of the time, so too is "Wall Street Week with Louis Rukeyser)."

In the early days of television, there was almost always an "extra" on stage whose role it was to fix whatever technical difficulties arose. Replacing a bad microphone, adjusting the lighting or the teleprompter, even supplying cough drops to a coughing panelist, or making sure that the right camera is being used—all of these things are important to a smooth running program. The lady who currently has that job, Natalie Seltz, is the same person who performed it on the very first program; she is a television director and producer in her own right and is well trained in the technical aspects of television, something the viewer may not observe but which is, nevertheless, important.

Speaking of technical television, there is a large production staff for "Wall Street Week." It consists of a producer, a director, sound and camera specialists, a floor director, a graphic artist, and a staff of various specialists including clerical help. In addition to shooting the actual half hour show, there are a myriad of details surrounding the production of such a program, and it requires more people than many would imagine. Television programs do not just happen; they must be planned, orchestrated, and managed well before the night of broadcast, and on an ongoing basis.

There have been several producers of the program, but the one who has held the position longer than anyone is the current producer, Richard DuBroff. He is responsible for virtually every aspect of the production, from planning, interviewing potential special guests, and scheduling panelists to processing mail from the viewing public, negotiating details for remote broadcasts, and supervising virtually everything connected with the program. Without an energetic, hard working, and dedicated producer, no television program can be successful for very long. And Rich DuBroff is all of these things.

We have had so many programs that it is difficult to pick one or two that stand out above the others. Each of them has been an experience of one kind or another. Some have been good, informative programs; a few, in my humble opinion, have not. But I truly believe that in its totality "Wall Street Week with Louis Rukeyser" has served several important functions. First, it has educated the public about economic and investment trends and events. Next, it has brought before the public, leaders in the investment, social, political, and business worlds. Finally, "Wall Street Week with Louis Rukeyser" has been a pioneer in economic journalism, with a far greater audience than any or all similar programs. Its future will continue to be bright because it provides a valuable public service particularly to the investing public.

Of recent vintage, there were two programs for which I have fond memories, one in which I participated and the other in which I did not.

The former was a special program which aired in November, 1990, commemorating our twentieth anniversary. This program was broadcast live with a live audience direct from the Tavern on the Green in Central Park, New York.

Over 300 people were in attendance, representing friends and families of most of the cast of the show plus many of the outstanding guests of the program over the years. That was, indeed, a memorable evening during which we reviewed the past and discussed the future. In addition to being fun, it was interesting and somewhat nostalgic to look back at the hundreds of times we had broadcast. Along with my friend and long-time associate, Frank Cappiello, I was fortunate enough to participate on the program. So, too, did Peter Lynch, the acknowledged number one money manager of the decade of the 1980s and John Templeton, probably the most successful money manager of all time. And we had a chance to renew acquaintance with our very first guest, Stan West. I hope our viewers enjoyed that program as much as I did because, for me, it represented two decades of involvement.

Another highlight for me was a program in March, 1991 during which Frank Cappiello and I were "inducted" into what is known as the "Wall Street Week with Louis Rukeyser Hall of Fame." Theoretically, the members of this small club are those whom the viewers of the show consider their favorites. Whether or not this is true is a moot question. But, at least that program represented public recognition for a job well done. Was it merited? I will reserve judgement on that, but it was good to become a member of such an elite group of people, which until that time consisted only of Malcolm Forbes, Peter Lynch, John Templeton, and Merryle Rukeyser (Lou's indomitable, fascinating, and loveable father).

"Wall Street Week with Louis Rukeyser" has been, is, and (I hope) will continue to be an important part of my career and life. It has opened doors for me, it has helped me meet many fascinating people and, from it, I have learned more than one book could ever contain.

the basics

chapter

how to be
a successful
investor

All of us want to be successful in the management of our money. Over and above everything else, I have three pieces of advice on how to be a successful investor.

OWN SOMETHING

I moved to Florida in 1977. At that time I lived in Miami and had an office with a spectacular view that overlooked Biscayne Bay. During those years, I recall several of my clients coming to my office and saying, "Carter, don't put any of my money in the stock market; I can't stand it, it's too speculative, stocks fluctuate up and down, I can't sleep at night, and furthermore, I don't get as much income as I can from other investments." They would usually conclude by saying, "I want my money safe."

On those occasions, I remember gesturing out to Biscayne Bay and asking these clients, "Do you see all of those yachts out there?"

They would nod their heads affirmatively.

I would continue, "Well, do you know who owns those yachts? Those yachts are owned by people who either do or did own a business (or a share of a business), do or did own real estate (or a participation in real estate), or do or did own commodities."

Then I would point to another portion of Biscayne Bay and ask, "Do you see those row boats out there?"

Again, they would strain to spot the small dinghies bobbing in the water.

"Those row boats are owned by the savers and lenders of this world. So OWN something. It is the only way to become a yacht owner."

However anecdotal it may be, it is a point worth stressing.

BE CATHOLIC

I have a second piece of advice in the macro sense on how to be a successful investor. I say, "Be catholic." Note that the word *catholic* is spelled with a small "c." Also, recognize that I am not selling a religion or a pipeline to the Almighty. Instead, I am emphasizing long-term vision, goals, and a plan by which to reach those goals. It is important to stress the need for periodic flexibility to adjust to changing economic and market conditions, and to one's own set of personal circumstances, as they too may change. Being catholic also entails having a bigger vision and thinking of more than what may happen tomorrow morning. The word catholic really means focusing on the big picture.

BE OPTIMISTIC

I have never met a pessimist who made much money. Those who know me immediately recognize that my approach to investing is very optimistic. And while optimism sells fewer books than *The Day the DOW Died*, it is certainly a breath of fresh air to hear something positive about investing. Events have occurred in the stock market during the last 40 years which have devastated many investors. But although there has been a major economic crisis almost every year, it remains true that patient investors have consistently made money in the equities markets. So *somebody* must be doing *something* right.

Investing is not as complicated as some people make it, nor does it have to be an exercise in futility. Rather than dwelling on pessimism and aligning myself with the "gloom and doomers," my strategy is to "stun them with optimism." Instead of "One hundred on the DOW in 1992," how about "10,000 in 2010?" I made that prediction on "Wall Street Week," and I was serious when I said it. The startling thing is that this figure is not that optimistic. 10,000 on the DOW in the year 2010 is only a little bit more than appreciation of 6 percent per year compounded, and that does not factor in earnings from dividends.

So, own something, be catholic, and remain optimistic. Those who live by these tenets are on their way to investment success. All they have to do is get started the right way.

chapter 2

investor psyche

Getting started the right way involves several prerequisites, but vital and above all else, one must start with self analysis.

We are all different. It really is not important how we are, but it is important that we *know* how we are in order to adjust to offset our own idiosyncrasies.

A psychologist could (and some have done so) write volumes on investing. Why, for example, do some people continually lose money while others consistently make profits? Why are some people greedy? Why are others willing to remain in a stock which is losing value, rather than limit losses and cash in their chips? Indeed, one of the most underestimated components to making money in the stock market is proper mental conditioning.

When it comes to investing, it is a general observation that people are emotional when they should not be. Investing in the stock market should be an un-emotional endeavor. But people tend to either fall in love with a stock or hate it fervently. Investors should want to own a stock if they believe it will perform well for them and avoid buying it if they think it is going to under perform. It is best neither to love nor to hate where stocks are concerned.

Over the years, many elderly widows have said to me, "My husband loved that stock and he told me never to sell it." Well, never is a long time and I have learned in the money game that there is *never* a reason to say *never*.

That husband may have instructed his wife to avoid selling the stock because he wanted to avoid the tax bite on an accumulated capital gain. Indeed, if that husband were still alive, he might want to sell that stock if he could avoid the tax on it. So when he tells his wife, "I'll never sell that stock," what he implies is, "I'll never sell it *if I have to pay taxes on it.*" The poor widow, however, infers it as his directive never to sell, regardless of the income she may need. Frankly, this kind of common thinking is uncommonly naive. That woman should understand one basic tenet well-known on Wall Street: the stock does not know who its owners are, certainly can not reciprocate emotional feelings, and is not a better stock because of being loved nor a worse one for being scorned.

PATIENCE

If an investor has enough vision to see value in a stock, he should not necessarily expect it to jump in price the week after he buys it. People are discouraged when they buy a stock, and for whatever reason, it drops in value. If the reasons for buying the stock are good in the first place, then displaying some patience, staying with it, and even adding to a position if it declines may make good sense. Investors should avoid the trap of buying a stock to get a short swing out of it. Instead, they should buy because, over the next several years, they expect that stock to perform well. Conversely, if for some reason investors change their minds about that stock, and something occurs that makes them think it no longer holds the value they thought it would, then losing patience with the stock is also a virtue. It is far better to cut losses, get out and into something better, than stubbornly to hope for a sudden improvement.

VISION

Many people buy the buggy whip companies of yesteryear, instead of the emerging companies of the future. Having enough vision to recognize that times change and that different social mores exist is an important characteristic of thoughtful investors. It is best to be in the stock of companies that are going to be in the vanguard of what will likely happen in the future. For example, I am convinced that one of the great social and economic developments in this nation is going to be the rebuilding of the infrastructure. Investing in that area, *with patience*, will pay off. If, however, the economy is in a cycle where government cannot spend in this area, companies benefiting from such spending may not fare well. Having vision and patience to ride through short-term aberrations in the market is keenly important. Vision and patience are two sides of the same coin.

FLEXIBILITY

In volatile times, as in all market conditions, flexibility is important. Changing economic and market climes, as well as evolving personal financial circumstances mandate a flexible approach to investing. Today's good opportunity may be tomorrow's lemon. Times change, the economy changes, per-

sonal circumstances change, and one must be willing to adapt
to the times.

GREED

There is an old saying which some have bandied around for
years, which is still true today: "Bears can make money, Bulls
can make money, but Pigs can never make money." Everyone
wants to make a billion dollars tomorrow morning, and in trying to do so, people take unseemly risks. It is one in a million
who succeeds in making substantial money overnight. For this
reason, most people are well advised to avoid trying altogether. In attempting to pinpoint that one stock that will outperform all others, investors should expect failure. And if they
happen to hit the one situation in a million where their stock
lays the golden egg, they should recognize that their success is
due less to skill than to luck. It is certainly acceptable to let
luck have a chance, but to expect it or feel deserving of it is
folly.

I find that greed is all too common among investors. I
recall the early '60s, when we were in the midst of a great bull
market in technology stocks. One day, a fellow came to my
office, and he said, "I can afford to take a risk. I want to be in
the great growth companies of this world. You go ahead and
make the decisions on which stocks to buy. I know what I'm
doing and I can afford the risk." So, following his wishes, I put
him into several good scientific companies—Texas Instruments, Xerox, IBM, Polaroid, and other great growth companies of the day.

However, on this occasion, my timing was wrong and the
client lost money, blaming me for lacking the foresight to know
how those stocks would perform over the short term. In other
words, he was asking for the impossible. He wanted to be in

those stocks, and he clearly understood the risks. But this is where his responsibility ended. Within weeks, he lost enough money to persuade him to liquidate. Greed, combined with his short-term bias, had completely subjugated the virtue of patience.

Greed directs investors into other realms of skewed thinking. For example, I often endure people decrying others who have made money by virtue of inside information. Yet, the irony is that these same people, if they are my customers, *hope* I have inside knowledge. This omniscience is one reason they place their trust in me, and I am certain that they hope every broker with whom they deal has inside information *even though* they know acting on such information is illegal. Their thinking is, "I don't want *that* guy to make money on that information. He should share it with the public—meaning *me*—so I, too, can realize the benefit of that illegal act."

FEAR

Fear is a common characteristic instilled in investors from the first time they call their broker to place an order to buy a stock. Those who are afraid of the market, or those who worry they are going to lose money, have no chance of long-term success in the stock market. If investors are in stocks in which they have faith, they should not be afraid and should not fear a crash, nor the possibility of losing all their money. In fact, losing all of one's capital in the stock market is a rare occurrence. Contrary to prevailing thought, bankruptcies are few and far between and very few stocks ever lose 100 percent of their value.

Those who fear what the market might do display insufficient stamina to wait for a stock to gain in value. Consequently, they also stand little chance of making money. By contrast, those who have faith in the market over a period of time are the only ones who have a chance to profit, and they can expect an above average return on their investment.

HUMILITY

Humility is the glue that joins together all of the disparate components of an investor's psyche. Anyone who has been involved in the investment business for any sustained period of time has developed this trait. What strikes me about the psyche of successful investors, particularly as it relates to the matter of humility, is that many of the best money managers, including those who appear regularly on "Wall Street Week," are some of the most self-effacing men and women in the world, who fully recognize their strengths and weaknesses. The Templetons and the Lynches of the world exude humility. The smart ones say they know little about timing or what the market may do next week or next month. The common denominator is that they all recognize value. They admit they know little of what the short-term outlook on a stock price may be, but they know whether a stock represents good, long-term value.

Another common denominator is that they all know they are fallible, that they can make mistakes. My good friend and associate, Frank Cappiello, said on "Wall Street Week" that if he had learned anything over the years, it was humility. And that, coming from a consistently successful investment advisor, is wise advice for anyone.

chapter

3

creating
investment
goals

The most important part of money management is the creation of an eventual goal for a given portfolio. And goals vary considerably. But just as no one would go to an airport to fly an airplane oblivious of where it is going, neither should an investor plunge into the market without having some idea of a financial destination. It is almost impossible to accomplish something without having any idea what that something is.

In the very beginning of any investment program, it is axiomatic that investors should determine what they are trying to accomplish. People who come to me asking for my advice on how they should invest their money have usually never thought through what they are trying to accomplish.

A CASE IN POINT

Several years ago, when I lived and worked in Miami, a lady called to tell me she had a financial emergency. I didn't know what she meant by financial emergency, but by the end of our brief conversation she had convinced me that I had to see her right away. So I canceled my appointments for the day and went to meet her. When I arrived at her house and inquired about the nature of the financial emergency, she replied, "Well, the emergency is that my husband has left me."

That, in and of itself, did not strike me as either unusual or worthy of the urgency of her request. But she continued, "I am less concerned that he has left me than I am by the settlement: the real problem is that he has left me a spending allowance of *only* $50,000 a month!" (She pointed out that this sum was not alimony, but an after-tax spending allowance.) When she regained her composure, she threw up her arms in exasperation and said, "I don't know how I'm going to get along, that's just not enough money to survive."

When I asked whether she had any alternatives, she replied, "Well, yes, there are two things that I can do. First, I can release one of my seven secretaries. The second alternative, God forbid, is that I can spend some of my *own* income!"

This story, while surrealistic to some and humorous to others, illustrates two points. First, a lot of money to one person may not be much to another. Many people say to me, "I don't have much money—*but* . . ." When they say this, I don't know whether they have $20,000 or $20 million because, in either case, they usually never think they have enough. I, however, take the view that whatever somebody has is a lot of money, because it is 100 percent of what he has, and 100 percent is a lot.

The second point evident in this story is that this woman never took time to establish investment goals until the task was

suddenly and unwittingly thrust upon her. When I ask clients
to identify their goals, they will instinctively dish up the conventional response. "Well," they say, "my goal is to make a lot
of money." I consider that a lame response. Making money is
a means to an end, and making a lot of money is a very vapid
goal, fraught with peril.

If I try to show them the error of their ways, they retreat
until they have conjured up what they believe is the answer I
want to hear. "OK, let me tell you what I want," they reply, "I
want a good rate of return on my money." In all likelihood,
they are unsure of what they mean. After all, what *is* a good
rate of return? Is it 5 percent? 10 percent? 20 percent? Just
what is a good rate of return on one's money?

RULE OF THUMB

My answer to this question is basic, yet accurate: A good rate
of return on one's money is whatever is made *net* of inflation
and taxes. If someone makes 10 percent on his money and he
pays taxes of 30 percent, he will be down to 7 percent. If, over
the course of a year, the value of that capital has declined by 4
or 5 percent because of inflation, he will have really made a net
of 2 or 3 percent, which is not a very satisfying rate of return.

Put another way, if an investor places $1,000 in the bank at
an interest rate of 10 percent, he makes $100 per year on his
money. If taxes reduce that by 30 percent, he has now made
$70. But, if the purchasing power of that original $1,000 declines by 4 percent each year, he has lost $40 worth of purchas-
ing power and has really made only a 3 percent rate of return
on his money.

If a money manager says, "I'm going to make for you,
after taxes and inflation, 3 percent on your money," you will
begin searching for another advisor. But if the manager says,

"I'm going to make you 10 percent on your money," this is music to your ears. The truth, however, is that both statements yield the same results.

CLIENT EXPECTATIONS

Some of my clients tell me that they want not only a high rate of current income return on their money, but also capital appreciation. When I ask how much, they reply, "Well, as much as you can make." Then I continue, "What would you consider an acceptable annual capital appreciation?" Inevitably, there is a long silence as the client has no standard for determining a good or bad rate of return.

The only *real* rate of return on money should be the rate on a "total return," the income *plus* the capital appreciation, minus the depreciation made in any period of time. This is the *only* way to invest.

People will say, "I want to do all of this, but I want to take as little risk as possible. In fact, I don't want *any* risk. I want to make sure that my capital is not eroding in value." To make a high rate of return on one's money but to take no risk is almost an impossible task. And in these times, risk is *real*. Some say, "Oh, well, I understand that. I'm willing to take some risk." But when they *do* take the risk and lose money, they discover that they underestimated the risk they wanted to take. Many, even the affluent, have a passbook mentality— "Money *ought* to earn a rate of return on a constant basis, and I ought to have some way of guaranteeing the results." Indeed, this can be accomplished, but not with the kinds of results that people want. High income and good capital appreciation with no risk is a tall order.

There is still another common response. Some of my clients will say, "I want to outperform the market. If the market is up 20 percent, I want to make 25 percent. If the market is down 20 percent, I'll be happy if I lose only 15 percent." This, also, is a vapid goal because it then becomes a game of battling against the market rather than trying to accomplish some defined objective.

OFFENSE—DEFENSE

I like to explore with my clients the eventual use of their money and what they should be doing with that capital. In a good portion of the cases it becomes a combination of requiring money on which to live but also building capital for the future and for eventual retirement. This is the mainstream of investment philosophy for most people.

Investors should have a well-thought-out strategy. They should say to themselves, "I have X amount of capital, I currently need Y amount of money on which to live, and I eventually want to have Z amount of capital because I'm going to need that on which to exist as I grow older." If I can bring people to this conclusion, I feel better about the advice I dispense.

Therefore, before making any investment decisions people should, quite literally, establish a long-term budget for their assets. They should painstakingly determine the extent of their assets, their liabilities, their income, their expenses and then construct a long-term budget bearing in mind several assumptions. These assumptions should include factors such as inflation and interest rates, rates of return on their money—both capital and income—and assumptions on their future lifestyle. These assumptions are *not* complicated for most people, and this is why I shy away from those who say, "Look, don't bore me with the details. I'm going to give you an amount of money, and I'm going to see what you can do with it. If you do well, I'll give you some more. If you don't, I'll pull it and find another money manager."

My rejoinder to such a person is that his goals are insufficient for me, because I will always question whether I am doing the right thing for the client. Furthermore, I am not a swinger in the market and I contend that most people should not be. Serious investors should have a true purpose, a valid goal, and a coherent plan by which to arrive at that goal, and they should invest as speculatively or as conservatively as their goals demand.

A CASE IN POINT

I have a client who is ninety-five years old. He is in reasonably good health for a ninety-five year-old but is understandably not up to the task of playing a dashing game of tennis each day. This client happens to be 100 percent invested in bonds, the income of which is in excess of his current spending needs on an after-tax basis. He has chosen to invest his money conservatively. But the purpose of his investment strategy is to ensure that there are funds available to cover his living expenses for the rest of his life. His life expectancy is actuarially no more than three years, perhaps less; actuarially, life is never really over.

Given his situation, why should he endure high degrees of risk with his money which, over a short period of time, he might lose? Why negate the possibility that he will continue to live a comfortable life? This man has problems similar to other people, which include a higher cost of living each year and, in his particular case, medical costs which comprise the bulk of his spending. I see no reason to worry about too many esoteric, long-term exigencies for him. Instead, it is a simple matter of making sure that he is invested in high quality assets that can be expected to support him for the duration of his life.

This man also has a secondary objective, and that is to leave something to his heirs. In his particular case, the heirs are well off, so building capital is not his most important goal. In the end, after analyzing his situation and goals, I conclude that I should avoid taking high short-term risks for him and, instead, produce above average current returns, albeit returns "locked in" for the foreseeable future.

Moreover, I conclude that the client is not an extremely wealthy person. For this reason, I recommend that all of his bonds be taxable, the main reason being that a big part of his spending is on medical care, which is fully tax deductible. Therefore, after factoring in his current medical expenses, he pays very little tax. Although by some standards he has a high level of current income, he does not have to pay taxes because the big bulk of his spending is tax deductible. Thus, I have placed him in taxable bonds which offer a high cash return. Admittedly, most people are not 95 years old and most have longer term horizons than does my client. But this is an example of a goal which is easy to attain, without incurring inordinate risk.

Finally, after analyzing his disposable income, I conclude that it is currently in excess of what he needs. Therefore, he is somewhat protected against future expenses because he is able to re-invest some of his income. In short, his is not a difficult portfolio to manage, but the strategy, from the outset, is based on what we are trying to accomplish. We are responding to his needs, rather than reacting to immediate events.

ANOTHER CASE

Several years ago, I worked with a trust company of a bank in Baltimore. One day, a gentleman walked into our offices and told us that he had 14 grandchildren and that he wanted to create a trust sufficient to educate them through private school and college. He gave us the ages of the grandchildren and told us to structure a comprehensive strategy to fulfill his request.

It was our task to calculate how much money he had to place into this trust so that when the last grandchild graduated from college he would have completely funded their education, simultaneously depleting all funds in the trust.

The bank assigned me the task of coming up with some assumptions, and I made several, including the rate of return on his money he could expect each year, the amount he had to spend each year based on the ages of the children, projections of what school and college expenses would be, and so on. I finally came up with a figure of $350,000 which, at that time, was roughly $25,000 per child.

I lived to see the last child graduate from college, with $5,000 to spare in that trust fund. On the surface, mine was a stellar performance of balancing goals and assumptions. But before I boast about how clever I was, let me add that I made two mistakes along the way. First, I underestimated what the rate of return on the money would be over that period of time; second, I also underestimated the cost of education.

The interesting thing was that one error offset the other, resulting in no net change to the bottom line. The money earned a rate of return more than I could have envisioned, but the money was worth less than I could have envisioned. The result was that my conclusion was correct, but my reasoning flawed. This is an example of the kind of planning process everyone should undertake, making assumptions as to what the future may bring. Even if the results are slightly skewed, the discipline is in place to allow for changes along the way.

A COMMON GOAL

Having enough money to cover retirement is ultimately what most people try to accomplish with their money. Most want enough to live independently for the rest of their lives. This is not necessarily an achievable goal by everyone, but it brings into play several additional considerations. First of all, do I have sufficient capital to produce that goal? Second, what kind of financial life am I going to be leading at the time I *do* retire? And third, what other sources of income or assets will I have at my disposal?

On this latter subject, most people overlook several items when they search for what is available to them upon retirement. Social Security is obvious. There are stated benefits from Uncle Sam, and one can extrapolate what the future benefits will be, based on general assumptions of inflation. However, retirement benefits from employers are not always so obvious and are sometimes very unpredictable. Some have pension plans which pay fixed benefits upon retirement, while others have money purchase plans which not only pay variable benefits but do not necessarily have predictable contributions.

There are other sources of assets that people sometimes overlook. Many have assets that they don't know they have. Or, if they know they have them they don't think of them as investible assets. Take the home, for example, which for most people is the pinnacle of their asset base. Most likely, it is an asset which is increasing in value, not necessarily because of inflation and real estate prices, but because homeowners are steadily increasing equity in their homes through mortgage payments. They increase their equity, even if the equity itself has not increased in value. Furthermore, the home in which they live during their middle aged years is not necessarily the home in which they may want to dwell during their retirement. In many cases the home in which they live during their middle-aged years is more home than they need or want when they retire. Here, then, is another available source of capital on which to earn a return upon retirement.

Incidently, Congress has been considering various changes in the tax code concerning capital gains on the sale of a primary residence. The current law allows homeowners who are fifty-five years old or more to deduct $125,000 of capital gains on the sale of a primary residence one time. The proposed amendment would either increase this deduction to $250,000, or eliminate the loophole altogether. As it now stands, however, this is a benefit that many people either do not know about or have not used.

If a husband and wife have lived in a four-bedroom house during the years of child rearing and, all of a sudden, those children have grown, matured and moved away, leaving an "empty nest," the couple probably will not require a fourbedroom house. Sentimental though they are, from a practical point of view a two-bedroom house would probably serve them well. And the availability of the one-time capital gains exclusion on a primary residence is a very big item for such homeowners. They can sell their home, pay little or no tax on the gain, buy another home, take down capital (or pay off the mortgage) from which to enjoy a rate of return.

There are other assets which people do not readily categorize as assets that they can turn into earnings. For example, I will facetiously tell clients that the silver service packed in the box in their attic is really money in the bank. Let's assume it is worth $2,000. If money was compounded at 10 percent annually and if the client sold that silver service for $2,000, he could invest the money and earn $200 per year. The reality is that people might as well be paying a fee to a storage company to hold that service, because it has value that the investor is not going to use. Certainly, there are all sorts of sentimental reasons for holding such items. But, sentimentality aside, how many people readily view a silver service as $200 a year—or $16.77 a month—for the rest of their lives?

Other hidden assets of which investors should be cognizant might include everything from works of art to antiques. To the extent that a piece of art work has value, and to the extent that if the owners sold it they could earn a return on it, by not parting with it what they are doing is paying every month to look at that work of art. If it has worth to them, fine.

But if they can live without that art, and if they are not going to notice it, there is another source of capital. Jewelry is still another example. If the person likes it, uses it and wears it, fine. But if the jewelry sits in the safe deposit box, never to be used, then why not have the valuables earning income?

And the examples could continue indefinitely. There are, of course, trade-offs between the ability to make money and the way a person chooses to live. It will be ever thus.

TOTAL RETURN

In planning and long-term budgeting, most people should focus on earning a total rate of return on their money. It makes no difference whether this return derives from capital appreciation, income, or a combination thereof. Following from this, investors should have a goal to accomplish that which they want to accomplish, over a long period of time, rather than overnight. In the investment of money, I suggest maintaining at least a five-year time horizon. Why five years? Because, on average, every five years the economy suffers a recession and possibly two. Therefore, a five-year perspective enables people to plan average earnings above the valleys of the bad years but under the hills of the good. A five-year perspective is an economic cycle that allows for realistic, long-term growth.

ADJUST FOR INFLATION

Another goal of most investors should be some degree of protection against inflation. This protection should be against not only the increased cost of living, but also the decreased value of capital itself. A study of the history of inflation in the U.S. over a long period of time reveals that it has averaged roughly 3 percent, with the last couple of decades averaging considerably higher than that; most prognosticators predict an average in the future of somewhere between 4 to 5 percent. Therefore, I make the assumption that from a practical point of view, inflation will be five percent per year.

There are two ways to protect against inflation. The first is to be invested in assets that offer capital appreciation. The second is to be invested in assets which generate income, a good portion of which can be reinvested. Fixed-income investments will lose to inflation if the income is spent. Therefore, converting income into capital and producing capital appreciation are the only two ways of offsetting inflation. To accomplish this annually (5 percent net after tax) is not so simple as most people presume. It cannot be achieved, for example, with a savings account, nor with corporate bonds or tax-exempt bonds if much of the income is spent. It is also impossible with common stocks unless there is capital appreciation in addition to income. My conviction is that equity instruments are essential to produce a sporting chance of offsetting future inflation. In short, stocks are the only way!

chapter

five stages of financial life

As I have already said, when I ask people about what they are trying to accomplish with their investments, they invariably respond "to make money." There is little debate that making money is a goal, but quantifying just "how much money?" and "by what time?" is essential to setting credible financial goals, and investors should have different goals and different time horizons, if only because of age.

For most people, there are five fairly obvious stages of financial life.

PREPARATION

First, there is the stage in which one is preparing for life in general. At this point, a young boy or girl is not yet a wage earner and has not really started being a "doer" of anything. This stage falls between birth and the conclusion of formal education, when one actually goes to work.

At this stage, the odds are good that the great majority of people have neither any other sources of income nor capital. However, it is a very important stage because how one is trained and manages whatever money he has may set a rhythm for his future financial decisions.

For instance, take the very early stage of life. A young man would like to make a little money in his spare time, so he decides to set up a lemonade stand on the corner. Or, he is a bit older and he decides to go into the lawn cutting business. This is his first entry into the world of capitalism and into the world of making money. When he enters into the lemonade stand business or into the lawn mowing business, he discovers that these businesses themselves require capital. They also involve expenses, they have revenue, and realize either profits or losses. If a child can be made aware that the lemons and the sugar cost something, as does the lawn mower and the fuel to run it, the youngster has learned a worthwhile lesson that may have lasting effects.

At that very early stage of life, if a person can begin to recognize that those businesses, simple though they be, require capital and labor, involve operating expenses, receive revenues, and produce profits, he or she will be on the way to understanding the system under which we live. Many parents underestimate the importance of these seemingly simple lessons and, consequently, fail to train their children to think in like manner.

Children should be taught things such as:

"I, your parent, will lend you the money to buy the lemons and sugar, the crate that you are going to put it on, and the cups to pour it into. But you are going to have to pay me back from your profit. Therefore, your capital costs you something. And if the lemonade costs two dollars to produce, and you receive revenue of four dollars, you pay your debt of two dollars back to your parent and you keep the remaining two dollars. What you should do next is pay your laborer (yourself) one dollar, and put the other dollar aside so that next time you open a lemonade stand, you have some start up capital."

This is overly simplistic, of course, but parents should endeavor to instill such thought progression into their children. If parents can instruct children that they should not spend all of the revenue, but plow some of it back into the production of more revenue, children will have learned a valuable lesson.

WAGE EARNER

The second stage of economic life commences when, for the first time, a person begins to earn a living. I contend that at this juncture, which begins in the early or mid-20s, depending on how much education one actually completes, the person is making more money than he will ever make for the rest of his life.

It may not be more money in terms of actual dollars, but it is all "gravy." From a life of having no money, it is a big leap to having some. And, for most, it is a stage of life when responsibilities are low and, therefore, most funds are spendable or investable at the discretion of the person. Whatever is made is a bonanza, and it is at this stage where the ability to put aside some earnings to create capital which, in turn, should produce even more earnings and capital, is at its zenith. Unfortunately, many new wage earners are also heavy consumers, not yet aware of the value of capital accumulation. Sure, they should enjoy the fruits of their labor, but saving and investing some for the future will hold them in good stead.

FAMILY FORMATION

Then there is the family formation stage of life. This not only includes marriage and child rearing, but also the purchase of a home, maintenance of a family, and all of the expenses attendant to these necessities.

Presumably, as a person matures in his profesion, he is earning more. But it is true that he is also forced to spend more to maintain an established standard of living. This is the longest and most lasting stage of economic life, the one in which the person is either successful or not.

During this period, it is vitally important to build capital, difficult as it may be. Without ever being conscious of it, most people *do* build capital at this time. Such things as making mortgage payments, accruing Social Security benefits, vesting in employer retirement plans, and so on, are ways in which individuals and families build capital for the future.

RETIREMENT

In time, retirement approaches. Whatever one has accumulated during his life through retained earnings, accrued benefits, or inheritance, becomes the nest egg for the rest of life. And the size of that nest egg will determine how the retiree will live. It is at this stage when the importance of building and having capital becomes magnified. It is all that is left.

DEATH

It may seem contradictory, but the final stage of economic life is death. It is the time at which the capital or sources of income which remain, becomes available to support a spouse, a child, or others who may be dependent on that inheritance. What is ultimately available will have a profound effect on those who survive.

In all stages of life, therefore, building capital on which to live a fulfilling and secure existence is important. However, it is unrealistic to expect the teenager or the young wage earner to begin preparing for retirement and death. But it is not unrealistic to advise the teenager to save and invest toward the purchase of a car; nor is it unrealistic to instruct the new wage earner to accumulate for the eventual down payment on a home. It makes good sense for the parents of young children to save capital for the high cost of college education; it behooves those in the latter part of their earning life to invest for retirement; and it is important for senior citizens to plan for death.

The important point is to acknowledge the wisdom of structuring an investment plan to meet the needs of the *next* stage of life rather than planning today from "cradle to grave." This is how people should focus their financial planning strategy.

the strategies

chapter

keeping up
with the
dow joneses

"Keeping up with the Dow Joneses" is the title of many of the talks I give throughout the country. In these discussions, I usually reflect on the current state of the economy—where it is and where I think it is going—and how government tax and spending strategies, along with Federal Reserve policy and world events may shape the economy and affect the average investor.

Much of my advice to investors revolves around the basic theme that stocks provide the best course to achieve the long-term goal of increasing real value of capital—meaning capital appreciation over and above inflation. Moreover, and contrary to popular opinion, stocks are also predictable.

While the past is not necessarily a comprehensive prologue of the future, a glance through history reinforces this
contention, at least if the investor holds good quality stocks,
employs patience, and is willing to ride through cycles. Furthermore, such a strategy does not necessarily require expertise
in stock selection or timing. Take the record of the Dow Jones
Industrial Averages over the last four decades, commencing
December 31, 1949 (See Figure 1).

The 1950s and 1980s were banner decades, proving to be
the best decades of this century for the stock market. The 1920s
just missed because of the free fall of the market in 1929. During the 1950s, as a result of recovery and meeting the pent-up
demand of consumers for goods and services after the supply
drought of World War II, stock results were electric. From the

Figure 1   Dow Jones Industrial Average

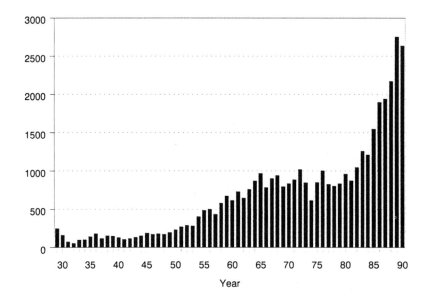

end of 1949 to the end of 1959, stock prices more than tripled. And virtually the same thing happened in the 1980s as stocks went from 839 at the end of 1979 to 2753 at the end of 1989.

Such was not the case in the 1960s and 1970s. Although the market performed very well in some of those years (1961, 1963 through 1965, 1972, and 1975 through 1976), the net capital appreciation in the 1960s was only about 18 percent for the average industrial stock, and in the 1970s, it was flat. Nevertheless, investors realized profits in both decades because dividends were substantial.

From 1950 to 1990, the Dow Jones Industrial Average went from 200 on December 31, 1949, to 2634, where the markets closed on December 31, 1990. Of course, the Dow did not move upward in a straight line; there were violent fluctuations during this period in both price and dividend yield. However, breaking down the period into five-year increments reveals a long-term tale of consistent periods.

In the forty-one years under scrutiny, there were thirty-seven five-year periods.

On a full-year basis, there were eleven years (25 percent of the time) when the averages actually declined, and thirty years (75 percent of the time) when they increased. A study of five-year periods shows that the averages were down seven times (20 percent), and up thirty times (80 percent). Of course, this represents only capital appreciation or depreciation.

But when dividends paid are added to capital appreciation, one discovers that there was only one five-year period in which total return was negative (See Figure 2). That was the five-year period from December 31, 1969 through December 31, 1974. This five-year stretch saw a decline of 184 points in the averages (from 800 to 616), offset by dividends totaling 170 points, for a net overall loss of fourteen points, or less than 2 percent. And even this loss would have been eliminated by systematic reinvestment of dividends. Therefore, there was *no five-year period* in 41 such periods during which an investor

Figure 2   Five Year Total Returns (%)
Dow Jones Industrial Average

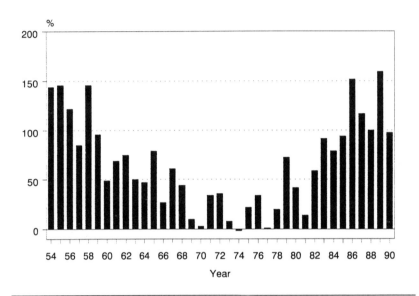

would have lost money by investing in the stock market average of quality common stocks on a total return (compounding of income) basis. This is a surprising and remarkable fact.

Average capital appreciation for the 37 five-year periods was 40.46 percent (about 7 percent per year compounded), and the average total return (appreciation plus dividends) was 67.16 percent (roughly 10 percent per year compounded). All of this was achieved *without* an assumption of the reinvestment of dividends, which would have certainly increased the total return considerably.

As for inflation as measured by the CPI (Consumer Price Index) during this time, it was nowhere near this level. (See Figure 3.) Sure, inflation was historically high during part of the 1970s and reached double digits (10 percent or more) during the early part of the 1980s, but it averaged a lot less than the return on stocks for most of this time.

Figure 3   Inflation Measured by the Consumer Price Index

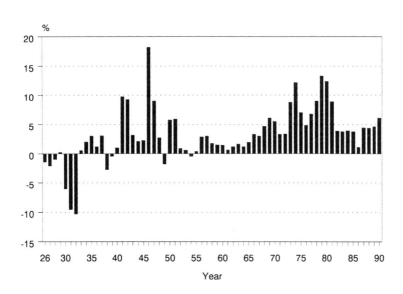

People tend to reflect on the past with short-term, recent memories, but contrary to those memories, inflation was not as high in this country over the last four decades, as we might assume. Although in recent years we have become accustomed to the cost of living increases in excess of 5 percent per year, this is not the longer term trend but, rather, an aberration. Consider the fact that Congress demanded and President Nixon reluctantly agreed to wage and price controls in 1971 to stem what was then considered a "horrendous" inflation rate of 4 1/4 percent, versus much lower rates during the preceding decades. It was not until the "guns and butter" economic policies of the Vietnam War that this nation experienced high rates of inflation.

Incidently, it was partially those very wage and price controls that precipitated the worst economic downturn (and stock market depreciation) during 1973 and 1974. Although many hope today that lessons were learned from these experiences for the future, we are still suffering economically from the legacy of the late 1960s and early 1970s.

Is relatively high inflation in this country here to stay? Probably and regrettably, it is. But history does point out that equities (stocks) are an offset to inflation; in fact, they are the only viable offset.

The fragility of other instruments can best be illustrated against the backdrop of recent history. Following World War I, Germany took drastic steps to stabilize its currency. Inflation ran rampant and people who had Deutsche Marks, or any instrument that promised to pay Deutsche Marks, lost substantial sums of money. In short, currency became worthless. Everyone will likely remember his high school history teacher discussing that during the war, Germans had to haul wheelbarrows full of Deutsche Marks to their local bakeries to pay for a loaf of bread. But what the high school teachers probably overlooked was that during the same period, tangible assets such as gold, gems, farmland, homes and stock in German corporations retained their value. German corporations, like Daimler Benz, continued to operate during the war and their stocks maintained value. Indeed, once the war ended, these stocks adjusted to inflation and eventually followed a normal recovery.

Bonds are an insufficient offset to inflation, even though bond rates today are higher than they have been historically. Some investors mistakenly believe that when they own a bond, they own something tangible; in fact, they own absolutely nothing. All a bond holder owns is an obligation by someone to provide money at some future date. A bond is an IOU, not equity; it is an instrument calling for money, but it is not a physical thing that one owns. In fact, some have gone so far as to suggest that so-called "zero coupon bonds," or discounted interest bearing obligations, are nothing more than conventionally acceptable versions of a ponzi scheme. These instruments may work for the investor, but they have no real value.

Bonds represent, in effect, legalized confiscation of capital. Not only do they pay fixed rates of return which are depleted by inflation, but also upon maturity the capital is depreciated in terms of purchasing power. And it is not hard to remember when bond income was less than inflation.

In the meantime, stock investors have been rewarded not only by capital appreciation but also by increased income virtually every year.

Granted, income returns in the form of dividends from stocks have been very low relative to the income returns available from bonds. There are many reasons for this, the most apparent of which is that corporations are loathe to pay out a large percentage of earnings in dividends. This is primarily due to the necessity of retaining earnings to enhance capital from which, in turn, better earnings are produced. There has been an increasing awareness that retained earnings is the cheapest way to raise capital, and contrary to the capital leveraging binge of the 1980s, most major industrial corporations are still paying out less than one half of earnings in dividends.

This augers well for the future dividend stream for stock holders. Not only do retained earnings help improve income and, therefore, subsequent dividends, but also dividend reductions are a rare occurrence, except for highly cyclical companies or those which pay out too much. Dividend increases are far more prevalent than dividend decreases.

To hark back to the long-term history of the Dow Jones Industrial Average, there has been a continuous increase in its value, with only brief interruptions. In fact, for the last 19 five-year periods under study (covering a time span of 20 years) dividend increases have occurred during each period, including the five year span ending in 1974. For investors, this is informative; it assures them higher dividends to use for spending purposes or for reinvestment. While in a given year (1991 was a good example), individual companies may reduce and/or eliminate dividends because of cyclical earnings problems or the need to preserve capital, the long-term trend in dividends has been and will likely continue to be positive, not negative. And that is the stuff of which inflation protection is made.

Many analysts view yields on stocks as a deterrent to better prices in the stock market, reminiscing on the better dividend returns of yesteryear. Indeed, they have a point, but I believe comparisons of this sort to the past are pointless and, at least to some extent, overlook not only net corporate cash flow from many sources but also the better coverage of dividends from earnings prevalent today than in the past. Investors can expect companies which pay out relatively small percentages of earnings but which enjoy better earnings, partially as a result of this very policy, to raise dividends even more in the future than they have in the past.

All of this leads me to conclude that, far from being speculative, good quality stocks are the only way to go for most long-term (even passive) investors.

chapter

risk

Risk is really in the eye of the beholder. All of us take multiple risks each day, although we rarely recognize them as risks, as such. When we cross the street, we are taking a risk, although we regard that not so much as a perilous trip as the achievement of a goal, namely to get to the other side.

And so it is with other things we do. I have logged millions of miles flying on airplanes, fully aware of the danger posed by such transportation. In fact, I reluctantly admit that I have always been a "white-knuckled" flyer, and for some very good reasons. Among them: (1) I do not understand aerodynamics; (2) it seems to me to be unnatural to be flying at 30,000 feet above the earth's surface; and (3) I have a profound fear of heights.

But my rational self tells me that flying is safer than most forms of transportation, that the odds of an accident are very low, that pilots are well trained, that there are built-in safety precautions, and so on. And, so, while I still have a fear of flying, I am also willing to fly because it is the only practical and expedient way to get from one place to another when traveling long distances.

Even the events we enjoy during our leisure involve risks. A tennis player risks twisting an ankle; a golfer shooting for the green risks going into the trap; a baseball batter risks being hit by the pitch; a bridge player risks going down at his contract because his bid is too high; a gardener risks losing an eye from a stray tree branch.

In an attempt to make money, there are similar risks. Having a job implies a risk of losing the job; owning a business includes the possibility of the business failing.

On and on we could go—essentially everything we do involves some risk. But we do what we do because there is also a reward in one form or another, and most of the time we focus on the task at hand rather than the associated consequences.

So, too, should be the case as far as the investment of money is concerned. There is a risk in every investment decision and action, but there are also potential rewards. The only true method of analyzing risk is to couple the degree of risk to the degree of reward, a statistic commonly known as the risk-reward ratio.

Several years ago, I taught a course on risk at the University of Wisconsin. I would start the course by listing on the blackboard various media of investment. They included the following:

- Common Stocks

- U.S. Treasury Bonds

- Corporate Bonds

- House

- Investment Real Estate

- Raw Land

- Collectibles

- Gold

- Commodities

Opposite those media, I listed various types of risks and/or rewards. Among them were:

- Continuity of Income

- Level of current income

- Possibility of capital appreciation (depreciation)

- Possibility of income appreciation (depreciation)

- Protection against inflation of the capital

- Protection against inflation of the income

- Marketability (liquidity) of the assets

- Cost of acquisition (sale)

- Cost of maintenance

I then asked the students to rank each asset category to the risk and reward categories on a basis of nine for the highest reward (lowest risk) and one for the worst.

Even before the ensuing classroom discussion began, the students would mathematically rate common stocks as the best value in terms of total score on a "total return basis."

Sure, there are other investments such as bank deposits, options, insurance, and closely held businesses. There are also other risks and rewards. But this exercise is a very over simplified way of assessing risk and reward, and serves to put into perspective the fears and aspirations investors have for the way they invest money.

Consider quality common stocks from the point of view of risk and reward.

First, consider continuity of income. It is rare, indeed, that dividends from stocks are not maintained. Sure, individual companies may periodically reduce dividends when earnings are hurt by cyclical or competitive pressures, but the mainstream of corporate objectives include regular and consistent dividend payments. It is certain that stocks produce income more consistently than any of the other investment media, with the exception of U.S. Treasury Bonds and corporate bonds; in fact, most of the other investment media pay no income whatsoever. In this category, I rank stocks a seven but would not quarrel with those who give them a six.

Moving to the level of current income, meaning the current rate of return, stocks in recent years have, on average, paid a rather low rate of return. But, as has already been shown, this low rate of return does not necessarily suggest a lack of ability to pay higher dividends. Rather, it is a conscious decision on the part of corporate management to retain earnings to provide capital for future growth in both earnings and dividends. I rank stocks a six.

For predictable capital appreciation versus possible depreciation in value, stocks again rate high, or at least, above the norm. The long-term record proves this to be the case. Although some will make a case that other media might perform better from time to time, most other investments incur extreme volatility, are subject to fads and fashions and, most certainly, are unpredictable money makers. Quality fixed income investments have low risk of capital loss but limited, if any, chance of appreciation (although they do fluctuate in price).

Likewise, real estate investments may produce attractive profits, but as we witnessed during the 1990-1991 recession, property prices can plummet in value. One of the perceptions of the risk/reward of stock investments is gleaned by the fact that stock prices fluctuate up and down not only on an annual basis but, literally, from hour to hour and day to day. Those who watch short-term quotes of stock prices get the impression that they are volatile, which really is not the case. I give stocks a five and could make the case for a six or seven.

The same type of analysis is possible for potential income appreciation versus depreciation, and here I rank stocks very high. Predictability of better dividends in the future is almost axiomatic, has historical precedence, and is as close to being assured as almost anything. In this category, I give stocks a nine, while recognizing that investment grade real estate also deserves high marks.

Since there is high predictability of both capital and income improvement, stocks obviously rank very high as far as protection against inflation. I score them at eight in each of these categories, although some may disagree. Indeed, in this area, I would not argue with those who would rank real estate investments higher.

In ranking marketability and liquidity, stocks deserve a nine. They are, quite literally, a phone call away from being bought and sold. There is almost always a ready quote, a willing buyer and a willing seller; the availability of liquidity is extremely high, not necessarily at the price a buyer is willing to pay or a seller is hoping to receive, but it exists nonetheless. Liquidity is even better for stocks than it is for bonds.

The last two categories, transaction costs and cost of maintenance, again warrant stocks a pair of nines despite the recent trend by stockbrokers toward charging higher commissions. But such commissions, sometimes amounting to as much as 2 percent of the value of transactions, are much lower than those charged by dealers in other investment media. Nominal commissions on bonds may appear lower, but there is often a wide spread between the "bid" and "offer" prices for bonds, mitigating their competitive transaction cost advantage.

And, of course, other media not only experience much higher fees and transaction costs of all kinds, but also incur enormous "mark-ups" or "mark downs" in prices and often require laborious negotiations even if willing buyers and sellers can be matched. Concerning maintenance costs, very few home owners or real estate investors are unaware of ongoing expenses including taxes, insurance, physical maintenance and billing (in the case of rental properties). This holds true for collectibles and gold in the form of storage costs, insurance and so on.

My total evaluation of common stocks in their various categories of risk and reward comes to an average of about 7.7. On a scale of one to nine this is high, and there is no other medium of investment that ranks higher.

Yes, there are risks involved in investing in the stock market, but the overall risks are lower and the rewards higher; at worst, the combination of the two is better with stocks.

Investors must assume risk in order to make money, and the perception of the risk involved in stock investing is overblown by many. In fact, relative to long-term investment objectives, one could say with impunity that there is really no risk in common stocks.

What still remains is the development of a comprehensive strategy for stock investments, and the establishment and management of a portfolio of stocks to minimize risk and enhance reward potential for investors.

chapter

diversification

The viability of the term "diversification" is debatable. A diversified stock portfolio is a desired goal for most investors but not necessarily for purposes of achieving maximum results. As a matter of fact, the more diversified a portfolio is, the less chance it has for superior performance. On the other hand, the under diversified portfolio runs the risk of mistakes in stock selection, resulting in poor performance.

Diversification is a popular subject of debate. It even garnered the attention of the Nobel Foundation, which in 1990 bestowed upon Dr. Merton Miller of the University of Chicago its prize for his pioneer work in the field of portfolio diversification. No question about it, diversification is important; but left unattended, diversification can soon reach the point of diminishing returns, becoming a counterproductive force.

I believe in diversification because I know I sometimes err in selecting stocks. But I also observe that through diversification, one major mistake will not prove fatal for an entire port-

folio. Diversification is, however, a defensive rather than of-
fensive tool. Putting all the eggs in one basket may be fraught
with peril, but if it is a good basket, the eggs will fare well.

How much diversification should an investor have in a
portfolio? The answer varies, but there are some basic guidelines. If a portfolio is invested in high-grade stocks, diversification is less important than if the stocks held are highly
speculative.

For a high-grade stock portfolio, I see no reason to own
more than, say, ten or fifteen different issues. I have always
believed in quality stocks, while at the same time recognizing
that speculative holdings might produce superior results.
Therefore, to the extent that some holdings are less than top
quality, perhaps owning a few more is not a bad idea.

One of the problems most investors encounter is the in-
ability to stay current with more than just a few companies. I
follow a long list of stocks and companies, but most investors
do not. For those who have less time to devote to stock analysis, a good piece of advice is to hold as few stocks as is "comfortable," to follow them closely, and to hold them if they
continue to promise good long-term results.

In fact, a good strategy for most investors considering purchasing a stock not currently in their portfolio is to consider
buying only if they sell a stock they already own. This is a way
of keeping a short list of holdings while concurrently compar-
ing them with other potential investments.

Admittedly, this flies in the face of the practice of many
institutional investors (in pension funds, mutual funds, etc.)
who are dangerously over diversified. This is sometimes due
to restraints placed upon these investors. Still other funds are
so swollen with capital that the managers have no choice but to
diversify, lest they control majority interests in hundreds of
companies. Because a fund manager might have to buy too
much stock of any one company to meet an investment objective, he will buy two, three, or four additional companies. This

is part of the fault I find with most institutional portfolios. They are over-diversified and the results of those portfolios are average, at best, and most often below average.

One person I know who successfully managed a highly diversified portfolio was Peter Lynch, who ran the Fidelity Magellan Fund during the 1980s. But even Peter agreed that he was over-diversified. There was no choice. He had too much money to manage, and he could not take even 5 percent of his fund's many billions in capital and invest it in one stock for fear that he would own too much of the company. He left the business at the peak of the market in 1990 saying he had done his thing; so, for the decade of the '80s he was a hero; for the '90s and beyond, it remains someone else's problem and opportunity.

In recent years, there has been increased emphasis on so-called "index" investing. Indexing refers to investing in all of the stocks in a given stock market index (i.e., the Standard & Poor 500), and was borne of a realization by many money managers that beating the market, performance-wise, was difficult and that staying with the market averages would, in the long run, translate to good performance. This may be true of the very large portfolios which are buying or selling securities but can be self-defeating due to the fact that they "make the market" in the stocks in which they trade. Of course, this is not the case with individual investors. Whereas the acquisition or sale of one million shares of a stock by a large investor can affect the price of the stock, an individual's purchase or sale of 100, 500, or even 1,000 shares has no appreciable effect on the market. In this regard, individuals have an advantage over institutions.

The really "big" money made by investors has been through the accumulation and holding of one or two big "winners." To the extent that such investments are diluted by mediocre or poor investments, overall results are diminished.

I recall a study made by the chief investment officer of a major trust company who analyzed the performance of individual accounts over a long period of time. To his amazement, he found that long-term performance was directly related less to the bank's investment policy than to its diversification activities.

He readily admitted that how an account was originally invested (which assets were "inherited") in the early years had almost everything to do with its long-term results. If, for example, an account was heavily invested in a good growth company, the performance of the account was good *despite* regular diversification moves. Conversely, if the account was originally concentrated in a "mundane" stock, despite periodic diversification into better growth issues, the performance was lackluster. Investors can learn from this study. Defensive investing can mitigate losses, but over-diversification can inhibit good investment results.

If owning the right stock at the right time is vital to investment success, how then should investors pick stocks?

chapter

the disciplines
of picking stocks

There are a few very simple guidelines that investors should use in selecting stocks, over and above their analysis of the types of businesses represented. If investors adhere to these disciplines, they may avoid major mistakes of selection, or at least, effectively be able to screen selections down to a few. Among these disciplines are:

1. Analysis of financial stability
2. Analysis of earnings growth potential
3. Analysis of dividends
4. Analysis of price

Investors can perform most of these analyses with a minimum of effort if they consult the various research services which are readily available. Companies such as Standard & Poor, Moody's and Value Line not only prepare written descriptions of the businesses of individual companies but also include in their reports useful statistics for those searching for past history and future projections. In addition to this, most brokerage firms can provide investors with future projections based on in-depth company analysis. Sufficient sources of information are available in most major libraries that subscribe to statistical services; thus, even if an investor does not subscribe himself, he can readily access any sort of information he desires.

Most of these services rate individual companies A,B,C, etc., in their ranking of financial stability. Admittedly, these ratings are often subjective judgment calls and subject to change, but they are based on analysis of the balance sheets of companies plus their ability to earn money. Most investors would be well advised to select stocks of companies rated highly by the statistical services. This may eliminate some companies which have good chances for profit potential even though their balance sheet may be highly leveraged. But for every one of those "lost opportunities," there is also a corresponding "lost risk."

Not all services provide information to analyze earnings growth potential, but some do. However, it is almost axiomatic to assume that a company which has displayed an above average increase in earnings over a long period of time is one which has the potential for repeating this in the future. A quick look at what has happened in the past can often reveal insightful clues about the future.

Aside from the rating services, the "information bible" of the investment industry is *The Wall Street Journal*. This publication offers all the economic news for making sound investment decisions, including plenty of discussion about industries and companies, along with intelligent insight on what people are thinking, both positively and negatively. Digested regularly,

The Wall Street Journal can be the most valuable aid for any investor.

The fallacy, however, is to allow today's news to influence every investment decision, and business journals tend to encourage this practice. What is the "hot" stock?" Who is the "up-and-comer" in corporate management, and how will he affect the industry?

Although regular reading of *The Wall Street Journal* is almost a must for serious investors, it is doubtful that impulse buying or selling as a result of having read one item in one article is a sufficient basis for investing. People should read and absorb information, and remember that acting quickly in response to something that *did* happen, is fraught with peril.

The first clue investors should attempt to uncover from rating services is the average earnings growth rate of a company. Of course, this varies according to economic cycles, but the average industrial company has historically had an earnings growth rate of between 6 percent and 7 percent per year compounded over a long period of time. To be considered a true growth stock, past and projected earnings should be 10 percent per year compounded or better.

Next, dividends are important. Investors should note that most companies pay out in dividends only a fraction of earnings. There are several reasons for this, but chief among them, as has already been noted, is the fact that the cheapest source of capital for a company is retained earnings. Borrowing money is expensive, and selling stock may dilute the results for stockholders.

If a company is to grow, it needs a constant infusion of capital, and retained earnings is the best source. Because dividends are the only tangible benefit that stockholders receive, investors should therefore want not only stocks which pay dividends but also those which have a history of increasing such dividends. The payment of dividends is not simply a matter of maintaining a regular cash flow, but it is a measuring stick to

help gauge whether or not management is really paying attention to the stock holder. Any company which is profitable but
pays no dividend is probably one whose management is ignoring its stockholders or believes the company is insufficiently
capitalized. If either of these beliefs reflect the thinking of
management, stockholders should beware. The most important consideration is not how much the dividend is but that it
exists and that management has regularly increased its amount
over time.

Of course, the price of a stock under consideration for purchase is a factor in deciding whether or not to buy. But it is my
observation that too many investors become too involved with
price. The public markets are as close to perfect as they can be,
and there are literally thousands of sharp pencils everywhere
trying to determine the "right price" for a given stock. Quota-
tions in the market reflect the collective judgment of those
sharp pencils, and it is difficult to second guess the market
itself. If an investor wants to own a stock for the long term
because he is expecting to double or triple his money, what
difference does it make—within reason—what price he pays?
A stock which an investor does not buy at $40 per share, be-
cause he thinks it ought to sell at $30 per share, is a stock that
makes no money for the investor even if it goes to $100.

However, there are some rules of thumb on this. As has
been said, the average earnings growth rate of companies is
about 6 1/2 percent per year. If a given market is selling at an
average of 13 times current earnings, the price/earnings ratio
of the average stock is about twice the growth rate. And so, on
that basis, an investor should pay no more than, say, 20 times
earnings for a stock whose earnings have been, and can be
expected to be growing at 10 percent per year. Of course, there
are all sorts of permutations and combinations in this kind of
analysis.

One thing investors should keep in mind about earnings
growth rate projections is that they are just that—projections,

not absolutes. Therefore, the higher the rate of annual earnings growth, the less predictable the numbers may be.

No company grows at an above average rate forever. Eventually, there is no room for further sales and profits. In its glory days, General Motors was a growth company, now it is cyclical; Sears Roebuck used to be a growth company, now it is mundane; even some electric utilities, which used to be called growth companies, are now defensive investments.

THE GAMMA THEORY

Several years ago, an economist analyzed the phenomenon of perpetual stock growth, and eventually formulated what became known as the "Gamma Theory." His basic premise was that no tree grows to the sky. Show me the greatest growth company known to man, and I will assure you that it will stop growing at its current rate at some point in the future. If corporate earnings generally are growing at 6 to 7 percent per year, and XYZ company's earnings are expanding at 20 percent per year, there comes a point at which XYZ cannot continue to grow at that level, or it will swallow the entire economy.

The economist coined this phenomenon the "gamma theory," in which he concluded that every stock will eventually tend toward the norm and that the great growth stock will eventually realize earnings growth tending toward the average. The underlying premise is that a high rate of earnings growth is more predictable for a shorter time period. The smaller the time frame one considers in the life of a stock, the less the risk of the price one is paying today; the longer the time frame, the greater the risk of overpaying. The Gamma Theory is a mathematical tool to determine whether one is paying too much for a company's stock.

I keep this intriguing benchmark in the back of my mind because it restrains the tendency to allow emotions to rule investment decisions. Every so often, I will spot a stock that appears to have high earnings growth expectancy and I become excited about the company. After working this theory into my decision, I eventually become loath to buy too much of that stock even though I may love the company. The price is discounting growth into eternity.

DETERMINING VALUE

If the price of a stock selected for investment seems to be too high relative to the market and/or relative to its prospects, investors should recognize three alternatives: one is to buy the stock anyway; another is to take a partial position in it and wait for it to adjust to a proper price; the third option is to invest in something else.

A stock's price relative to its earnings is certainly not the only criterion for determining value. Many would recommend other strategies. Dividend yield is one accepted guideline for judging price, as is price in relation to so-called "book value" or net asset worth. I do not disparage those who espouse these methods of valuation. They certainly have validity. But I do submit that the main reason investors should buy stocks is not strictly limited to the dividends which the companies pay. Dividends are important, but the main benefit of owning a stock is capital appreciation. And capital appreciation really depends on earnings or the ability to pay a dividend, not necessarily on the dividend itself.

The book, or net asset value of a company is very difficult to compute accurately. A stated net worth is almost always a recitation of original costs of assets, depreciated in accordance with tax laws, and then followed by a subtraction of the liabilities of the company. Such a stated net worth bears almost no resemblance to either the fair current value of assets or the earning ability of the company. There are, of course, exceptions to this, but to use stated book value as a method of analyzing fair market value is, in my opinion, an exercise in futility.

TECHNICAL ANALYSIS

There have existed and evolved over the years many techniques for analyzing and selecting individual stocks. Although I maintain that earnings are the main reason for the price of a stock over the long term, I recognize that there are many other ways to pick stocks. Recently in vogue (and reappearing from time to time) has been a system known broadly as technical analysis.

Although there are many varieties of such analysis, basic technical analysis concerns itself with a game of numbers as opposed to fundamentals. In technical analysis, there is a built in assumption that the market generally, and individual stocks in particular, have price momentum, and that this momentum will continue in a predictable direction unless an intervening force impedes its natural movement.

Therefore, technical analysts compute, measure, and chart price movements of stocks to discern trends. Using statistics such as the "200-day moving average," the "head and shoulders" formation of stock prices, the "gap" theory, and other such esoteric data, technical analysts believe that they can scientifically project future prices from past price movements.

Added to such "numbers crunching" are more statistics which compare stock price movements with many economic and investment numbers. Projecting market movements through an observation of such variables as the money supply, cash reserves held by institutions, the level of short positions, the volume of trading, the ratio of new highs versus new lows, and a myriad of other numerical relationships has become a fetish on Wall Street. With its increasing dominance in Wall

Street, it is my observation that it is becoming difficult to distinguish between true technical phenomena and self-fulfilling prophesies, which tend to rule the movement of markets regardless of traditional supply and demand dynamics.

I do not argue with the conceptual underpinnings of technical analysis. It certainly has some validity. It assumes that statistical relationships which have occurred in the past will be repeated in the future, and with this I concur.

But it is interesting to observe that scientific though technical analysis may be, there is almost always a large difference among technical analysts concerning the outlook for the market as a whole, as well as individual stock prices. The net result is confusion, and such confusion is far from scientific. Certainly, it would be pleasant to be able accurately to time purchases and sales, as well as stock selection, on a scientific basis. But technical analysis is, at best, only a tool, not a "be all and end all" to investment decisions. Trying to convert an art into a science is fraught with danger. For shorter term speculators in the market, technical analysis has its merits; for truly long-term investors, it loses much of its appeal.

A question which often arises in picking stocks is the appropriate emphasis one should place on the technical side of timing the market. The best advice to someone enamored with the latest bells and whistles which promise a "holy grail" for market timing, is to avoid the trap completely. Far better is the method of placing a discipline on timing. Reacting to what the market has done is preferable to anticipating what it will do. Therefore, timing should be based on hindsight rather than foresight. After all, it is true that hindsight is perfect, while foresight is subject to all sorts of error.

I have never known of a time when people have not said, "The outlook is uncertain." Likewise, I have never known a time when people have said "The outlook is certain." Unforeseen problems and unanticipated events can hurt a stock market, which is why I prefer to invest by hindsight rather than by foresight. More discussion of this will follow in the next chapter.

But it bears repetition that the long-term investor should "keep his eye on the ball," the ball being the longer term outlook for the market as well as for individual stocks. When all is said and done, the long-term outlook depends primarily on sales and earnings, and less so on "technical" indicators.

LEVERAGE

From time to time, leverage can be a valuable device for profiting from short-term moves in the market. But most investors, particularly those with less capital and those who pay little attention to their portfolios each day, are advised to avoid leverage altogether.

Leverage involves borrowing against assets in order to buy additional assets. An investor who places $10,000 with a brokerage firm to purchase $20,000 worth of stock is leveraging his assets. The brokerage firm acts as a bank, lending the investor the additional $10,000 of stock, charging interest on the balance.

A good rule of thumb for most people who apply leverage to their stock positions, is to make sure to pay less in interest on that margin than the cash income they are making on the assets themselves. In other words, limit the margin to available cash flow, or the capital may evaporate.

The Federal Reserve regularly reviews the margins allowable in the stock market and it has stood at 50 percent for some time. I suggest that investors borrow less than the maximum allowable; in a bad market, higher leverage can prompt forced selling to meet margin requirements.

Another rule of thumb that I use for margin is to plan to be out of margin at least once each year. This premeditated plan serves me well by forcing me to keep thinking about that margin. If an investor adheres to a fixed margin reduction schedule and is confident that his assets will produce more income than the cost of that margin, he should forge ahead and utilize leverage prudently. It is a tool to enhance performance, particularly for short-term moves.

TIMING

Having a discipline to time investments makes a great deal of sense, and there are several ways in which investors can exercise good timing.

First, after having selected which stocks to purchase, an investor can determine how much to invest in these stocks now and how much to plan to buy later, recognizing that the market will fluctuate up and down on a constant basis over time.

Regarding timing, the time to be in the market is always. Those who think they can figure out the right time to enter and exit are doomed to failure. Even if they are correct once, they have to be right twice, and so on. One mistake in the process can ruin the entire chain of trades, and so some prudence is required.

A so-called "collector" of stocks can offset the inevitable timing problems. This entails a predetermined strategy to buy either a fixed number of shares or a fixed dollar amount of stock periodically, regardless of price. This type of "dollar averaging" may not produce optimal results, but it assures that the investor will not buy all stocks at their temporary highs.

In summary, selecting stocks is not difficult if investors stay with quality. Emphasize holdings of stocks of companies which demonstrate above average growth of earnings potential as well as proven ability to produce such growth; exercise discipline in screening out stocks, utilizing leverage and timing purchases.

chapter

formula
investing

I have always been a believer in the system of money management known as formula investing. It is a strategy to offset volatility in the securities markets and while it does not necessarily guarantee maximum investment performance, it is an almost scientific way to offset short-term and even long-term swings in securities prices.

I recall the answer J. P. Morgan reportedly gave to the question "What do you think the market will do?" He replied, "It will fluctuate" and, of course, it always has and always will.

Before discussing formula investing, let me relate why I think it makes sense for me in particular and for most investors in general. I have confidence in my ability to forecast economic and social trends. It forms the foundation of most of my money management decisions, trying to discern whether or not to be heavily invested in various markets and also evaluating the viability of specific investments.

But anyone in the business of forecasting must, in time, develop some degree of humility. Logic, foresight, knowledge of what has happened in the past which may be a prologue to the future, and analysis of likely trends serves a useful purpose. However, unexpected events *do* occur which can defy conventional market wisdom.

To some extent, the stock market reflects the emotions of people in reaction to whatever happens. Sometimes there is euphoria in the marketplace and stock prices rise to levels which defy reasonable analysis. At other times stock prices plummet in response to bad news, and such declines are often unjustified.

I recall many such surprises. Among them are President Eisenhower's heart attack, the Cuban Crisis, the assassination of President Kennedy, wage and price controls imposed by Richard Nixon, the oil embargo, the Penn Central default, the cornering of the silver market, the invasion of Kuwait, not to speak of the one-day stock market "crash" in October, 1987. There are certainly many other examples of periods driven by panic buying and selling, such as the great bull markets of 1954 and 1955 and of 1975 and 1976. In fact, almost the entire decade of the 1980s saw stock prices higher than fundamental economics and corporate earnings could justify, due to a shifting of funds into financial equity as opposed to tangible equity.

In this century, the worst time in the stock market was the 1929 to 1932 era. Although I was alive and witnessed the carnage of the depression, I was certainly not a professional investor during those days. The era was devastating, highlighted by a bear market which lasted four straight years. The big crash occurred in October, 1929, but few people recall that for the year as a whole, the market was down less than 20 percent.

Then came 1930, which saw stock prices decline over 35 percent. This was followed by 1931 and 1932, when stock prices declined 50 percent and 20 percent respectively. Put succinctly, those four years were absolutely devastating, and investors in the marketplace lost whatever confidence they had in stocks.

It was during this period when people leveraged themselves to unseemly levels. With low margin requirements and people owning stocks on very high leverage, even a slight decline in the market caused a substantial drain on investors' capital.

It is unlikely that we will live through that kind of a period again in the foreseeable future. Several reasons bolster this conviction. Some basic structural changes are in place today which would obviate a market disaster of similar proportions. For one, margin requirements are much higher today, thereby discouraging the kind of speculation in the market that existed in 1929. In addition, the government has installed financial safeguards which did not exist then. Moreover, we have witnessed the emerging importance of the monetary system, as practiced by the Federal Reserve, and the development of many social benefits which produce income for people even in bad economic times. Social Security, job security, and various types of unemployment insurance are a few of the benefits that did not exist during those days. Most experts agree that these structural improvements would preclude a repeat of 1929.

There have been other tumultuous periods in the market. Not only have I lived through them, but I can vividly remember most. In 1948, I embarked on a career in the investment business, but my first exposure to a really poor market did not occur until 1962. Although it was certainly nothing like the markets of the late 1920s and early 1930s, this period wreaked financial havoc on many.

Strangely, however, the previous year was one of euphoria. The year 1961 saw a very strong market, with over-valued stocks and everyone thinking happy days were here again. Then things turned sour. By June of 1962, the market had declined considerably and chaos was evident everywhere.

I remember a specific date, May 29, 1962, which was the culmination of a bad bear market. On that day, the volume of trading soared, even though the stock market in those days closed at two o'clock in the afternoon. Without the high speed ticker tape that we have today, final quotes on that day were unavailable until 6:30 pm. There was absolute chaos, nobody knew the price at which his stock had sold, and it was impossible to get current quotes. It was a frantic scene.

I recall people were terror-stricken. But frightened though they were, they should have been buying stocks. A relatively young man at this time, I recognized this and was a big buyer of stocks during the spring and summer of 1962.

There is a saying, "When they raid the house, they take all of the girls, and the piano player as well." Likewise, when they raid the stock market, they take all stocks. *All* stocks decline. I remember looking at depressed stock prices and thinking, "I don't know what this market is going to do, but I think it is time to buy."

Then I made a mistake. I bought relatively conservative defensive stocks, including banks and utilities. Between 1963 and 1965, the market came back with three years of strong performance. While the defensive stocks rose in value, the really good growth stocks performed much better than the average, and I missed a classic opportunity. I learned from that lesson, and so, in 1966 when the market plunged again, I avoided a repeat of my earlier mistake. As a whole, the year 1966 was worse than 1962, with stocks down almost 20 percent.

At that time I reasoned that because stocks were down and I was still in those relatively conservative stocks, I was going to sell defensive equities and go into more aggressive growth stocks.

Then I hit paydirt. The years of 1967 and 1968 witnessed a strong rebound, and my growth stocks outperformed the market. I have observed the same pattern emerge in almost every major downturn in the market.

In my professional history, the worst period for the stock market through which I have ever lived, or ever hope to live, was between 1973 and 1974. In 1973, stocks dropped roughly 18 percent. In 1974, they sank another 25 percent, and there was panic in the marketplace. During that period, the stocks most affected were good quality growth companies, those highly leveraged firms whose price earnings ratios were high. Overpriced stocks, coupled with soaring interest rates, caused this decline in the market.

Due to an oil embargo, inflation was also soaring. Oil supplies were short, energy costs sky high, and the economy seemingly on the verge of collapse. Again, everybody thought the world was coming to an end, which it did not. In fact, during 1975 and 1976, the market came back strongly. Since then, we have witnessed several declines in the market, and also several strong markets.

The 1980s was a glorious decade, with few exceptions. In both 1981 and 1984, the market declined slightly. But the '80s saw one of the best performances in the stock market of all times. I should add that I do not think cycles are over, nor do I think fluctuations in the market have run their course.

We have witnessed violent fluctuations even during the good markets of the 1980s, with the result that most people have learned some important lessons. We have experienced fairly consistent fluctuations, some more violent than others, and have lived through booms and through recessions. We have lived through wars, both hot and cold, through the possible impeachment of a president, an assassination of another president, and turmoil in the Middle East. Each of these events can be devastating, with all variety of economic fallout. But in the final analysis, investors can draw intelligent conclusions from these experiences.

One conclusion is that although stock prices will fluctuate dramatically and melodramatically, equities will perform well for the patient investor. When I started in the business in 1948, the Dow Jones Industrial Average was roughly 177, and though I can only guess where it will close at the end of this century, the Dow has seen substantial long-term price performance, unlike most other investments. Over the same time investors have not only realized enormous capital appreciation, but have also enjoyed enormous increases in dividend income. Analysts and so-called stock market experts often overlook this when considering the history of the stock market. Indeed, statistics show that in 1990 the dividend paid was about 70 percent of the original cost of stocks in 1948. The 1948 investor has not only rocketed from 177 in the Dow Jones Industrial Average to 3,000 and higher in capital appreciation, but his dividends have returned that capital several times over.

Almost all of the unexpected events of the last century would have been difficult to foresee with either accuracy or certainty. And all of them brought about significant moves up or down in the investment markets.

It has often been said that the stock market does not like uncertainty, and those who are perennial pessimists have, over the years, consistently pointed out that "this is a period of uncertainty." The problem with this argument is that all eras include periods of uncertainty, the outlook is never perfectly clear, and although we should certainly worry about such things as government deficits, bank illiquidity, excessive inflation, over borrowing by consumers, economic cycles and market crashes, we nevertheless have to assume that excesses or traumatic events today will be offset by something else tomorrow.

Given the fact that foresight is, at best, only about 60 percent correct, what then is 100 percent correct? The answer is hindsight.

All people have the ability to know what has happened, and if they pay attention, they will always be correct about what has occurred. This is true of the stock market. It is easy to know what the market has done in the past, but less so to predict what it will do henceforth, at least over the short term.

Therefore, why not use this 100 percent accurate ability in the management of money? *This is where formula investing is valuable.*

Formula investing is simple. It is, quite literally, a way of arithmetically observing what has happened to the value of a portfolio and adjusting to it.

For example, assume an investor has a long-term goal of being invested, say, 75 percent in the stock market, 15 percent in bonds, and 10 percent in cash reserves. His portfolio has been established at those levels, individual securities have been selected, and the portfolio is in place.

The value of the portfolio and individual holdings will fluctuate both up and down on a constant basis. But if that investor has a predetermined system of adding to stocks when their value declines below 75 percent of the total portfolio, selling stocks when the value exceeds 75 percent, and adjusting bond and cash positions accordingly, he can mitigate against the inevitable and violent swings in asset values.

For sure, this is not a way by which to maximize performance. It certainly is not a way to buy at the bottom and sell at the top, but it is a way to guarantee buying low and selling high, and it eliminates a multitude of emotional reactions as well as major timing mistakes in purchases and sales.

Admittedly, this flies in the face of traditional advice many have proffered investors. Gerald Loeb is famous for advising investors to "let your profits run" and "cut your losses." While such advice is understandable, it does not recognize that markets and prices of individual stocks can and do rise and fall periodically for less than analytical reasons.

Of course, if a given stock performs well in the market, the odds are good that it will continue to do so; if it performs poorly, chances are equally good that momentum will carry it further downward. To some extent, I agree with Mr. Loeb.

However, if I have bought a stock or a group of stocks for the longer term and I am correct in my selection, I need not worry about interim fluctuations but am willing to take advantage of such fluctuations using a strategy of formula investing.

When a stock rises beyond my expectations, I am willing to sell a few shares and hope that I am doing the wrong thing because the remaining stock will continue to appreciate. On the other hand, when a stock or stocks that I like generally decline, this presents an opportunity to buy more at a lower price.

Of course, both precipitous appreciation and depreciation in value are a signal to me to reappraise my selection of holdings and even the percentage of funds I am willing to allocate to the market. This is where adjustment of my foresight takes over from the discipline of hindsight.

There are a myriad of different ways of applying formula investing, and it is impossible to enumerate all of them here. The main point is that such a discipline, predetermined, is invaluable to managing a security investment portfolio successfully.

DOLLAR AVERAGING

A variation of formula investing is the system of dollar averaging, on both the buy and sell sides. Again, this is a rather simple way of offsetting market fluctuations.

Under such a system, an investor determines what stock or stocks he should buy or sell but is unsure about precise timing. Or, perhaps, he has a predictable cash flow for investment purchases and/or for cash needs. He then decides to make periodic purchases or sales, either with a predetermined amount of money or with a predetermined number of shares.

Again, it is not guaranteed that the investor will buy at the low nor sell at the high. There is only one trade at the bottom and one at the top. But, at least he will avoid the mistake of paying too much or selling for too little.

Dollar averaging purchases are particularly advantageous for those who collect stocks over a long period of time in order to build equity capital through investment of cash flow coming from various sources, including income.

Likewise, dollar averaging is particularly advantageous for those who have a periodic need to raise capital or to spend funds by selling stock.

This is not a system for investors who pride themselves on having perfect insight with which to time transactions, but there are few who are capable of this on a consistent basis; virtually all who believe they are may be destined for disillusionment at some point in time.

Lest anyone believe that formula investing and dollar averaging are the tools only of the small investor, I point out that this is not so. As a matter of fact, these are the primary strategies that institutions utilize to invest their funds. Pension fund managers, managers of large insurance company portfolios, endowment funds, trust funds, and others have consistently practiced formula investing, albeit adjusting for common sense concerning a futuristic outlook and for analysis of the markets themselves.

One final thought on this subject is very important in view of a recent phenomenon in the market called "program trading." It has been said that program trading, meaning computer-driven programs designed to buy or sell heavily in the market as a result of market action itself by institutions, has rendered the stock market much more volatile than it has ever been.

The jury is still out on this matter. Whether or not the market, in the long term, has become more volatile is a matter of considerable conjecture. Perhaps program trading has done nothing more or less than adjust discrepancies in the market faster than has previously been the case. But one thing is clear. Short-term fluctuations have become more volatile, and rather than this being to the disadvantage of individual investors, it may be a help.

Large institutions which engage in massive block trading of stocks have an effect on the market itself and on the price of stocks they are trying to buy or sell. To some extent, then, this institutional trading can be self-defeating.

On the other hand, the average individual investor can expect to have little effect on the market through his purchase or sale of a few hundred, or even a thousand shares. By recognizing this fact, nimble individual investors can "dovetail" onto obvious program trading to buy stocks adversely affected by massive sell programs or sell stocks benefitting from massive buy programs.

For sure, program trading has an effect on interim valuations of stocks, but it does not appreciably affect the long-term outlook for the market or for individual holdings. As we have discussed, longer term stock prices reflect either earnings or expectations of earnings. Interim fluctuations present opportunity.

chapter

taxes

One of the more vociferous arguments of the day surrounds the issue of the capital gains tax and whether the government should tax long-term capital gains preferentially to the full income tax rate. There are credible arguments on both sides of this issue.

One line of reasoning suggests that profits are profits and investors ought to pay their fair share of taxes on *whatever* they make. This argument dispels the notion that there is any difference between making money through capital gains and earning it through current income.

A second line of reasoning maintains that it is unfair for the government to tax profits amassed over a long period at the same rate as money earned over a short time frame. Proponents of this view believe that investors who have held money over the long term have, to some extent, already been taxed by inflation. Such an argument is incontrovertible. A dollar earned in 1999 is a 1999 dollar. To tax that dollar at the 1999 income tax rate is fair. But to sell an asset in 1999, which an investor purchased in 1980 poses a problem. Indeed, the investor has made significantly less than the reported profit would indicate because he has earned profits in 1980 dollars, which presumably are worth less because of inflation during the interim.

Any discussion about taxation inevitably turns to the argument of fair versus unfair taxation. For example, why should I, living in Orlando, pay taxes to support a naval fleet based in San Diego? Why shouldn't the citizens of San Diego, who benefit directly from the increase in local business, bear the brunt of the cost of that fleet? Certainly, San Diego is realizing most of the economic benefit from those sailors' local spending habits. Why shouldn't local citizens foot the bill?

Of course it isn't fair. But what *is* fair? There has never been any such thing as fair taxation.

I maintain a couple of biases on the matter of a capital gains tax, generally endorsing the view that long-term capital gains—and it is a matter of how one defines long-term—should not be taxed at the same rate as short-term income. Two reasons bolster this conviction. First, as we have touched upon, capital gains have been taxed by inflation, while short-term income has not. Second, and even more important, the public stands to benefit substantially from a lower tax rate on long-term capital gains. It induces more risk capital into the marketplace, and it serves as a catalyst to spur the creation of new businesses and increase employment through capital formation.

However, just how much the discount on the tax rate should be is a matter of conjecture and debate. The fair thing to do (albeit an administrative nightmare), is what many people, including several congressmen have been suggesting. The equitable method is to zero out the inflation over the period of time that an asset is held. For example, if inflation averages 5 percent annually over a ten-year period, and an investor has held his asset for ten years, it is appropriate to tax only 50 percent of the gain. Likewise, if the asset is held for two years, then the IRS should eliminate 10 percent of the gain for taxation purposes (assuming, as I do, that inflation will average 5 percent per year).

This debate is evidently quite complicated as far as fairness is concerned. Developing a fair tax is, to some people, an impossibility. To still others, the concept of "fair taxation" is a classic oxymoron.

Even after employing all sorts of machinations on the subject, it remains true that our tax system has never been fair. Perhaps the only real solution is a flat rate for everybody as a percent of whatever he earns—no deductions or loopholes for anything or anyone. This is the only fair system if one believes that some people should have an opportunity to do better than others. If one does not agree, then theoretically at least, the tax system should reduce everybody to the same income level by an extremely graduated tax, thereby eliminating the incentive for people to make money and create capital.

The recurring issue in Congress concerning fair taxation (and whether to soak the rich) is a political red herring; it certainly spews forth political rhetoric from both sides. Nonetheless, it remains a fact that the middle class pays the bulk of the income taxes. What the government does to the middle income tax rate is really a determinant of whether Uncle Sam realizes increased or decreased revenue from the income tax. Proponents of the "soak the rich" bias always cite examples of the person who makes one million dollars a year. But the million dollar earner is a very small percentage of the population. Therefore, even if Uncle Sam doubles the millionaire's tax, the overall effect on total tax revenue is negligible.

Throughout the history of this debate, certain congressmen who have sought popular support have appealed to the "Robin Hood" character of the government—namely that government serves the function of redistributing wealth, taking from the rich and giving to the poor. However, it is debatable whether Robin Hood was the greatest man that ever lived. Sure, he stole from the rich to give to the poor. But, morally, is that right? Because I work hard, have ingenuity, and a good education, should I unwittingly be the victim of someone who slinks into my house and snatches my jewelry to give it to the indigent? The Robin Hood concept is not necessarily the greatest moral precept known to man. The fact remains that Robin Hood was a thief. We revere him because he helped the poor, but there is something fundamentally flawed with the concept unless one espouses the virtues of absolute socialism and champions the belief that everybody should share everything equally. We are witnessing the fallout of such untenable economic thinking in Eastern Europe.

TAX FOR CATASTROPHIC ILLNESS

One of the most controversial tax issues in the last few years has been the argument of senior citizens about catastrophic illness. At one point, Congress increased benefits under Medicare for catastrophic illness in order to provide for people who could not afford to take care of themselves for long lasting illnesses. The senior citizens of many states lobbied vigorously for the benefits, through AARP (American Association of Retired Persons) and other such organizations, and they eventually passed it through Congress. But when it came time to determine who would pay for the massive bill, Congress decided that it would charge what, in effect, was a user tax—that was to tax senior citizens who had excess income over the average. Suddenly, the same senior citizens who lobbied for the benefit, changed their minds. They determined it was unfair because those who required the benefits were not the same people who were paying the tax. The indigent were receiving the benefits and the affluent were footing the bill. That, they claimed, was unfair. Naturally, the conclusion at which seniors arrived was that it should come from the general public, not from them as a group. This was a perfectly understandable argument. Every one wants a benefit, but no one wants to pay for it.

SOUND TAX ADVICE

As for taxes, there are many things investors should consider in making investment decisions. I hasten to add, however, that there is no way that I feel qualified to codify *all* of the tax consequences of investment management. Suffice it to say that income taxes are here to stay, that changes in the tax laws will occur on a regular basis, and that investors should manage their money with an eye on the tax laws.

For the foreseeable future, it is hard to envision elimination of income taxes on dividends. From time to time some have made the statement that the taxation of dividends represents double taxation, first through taxation of corporate earnings and then again through the part of these earnings paid out in dividends. Altruistically, this makes sense. But the resultant loss of revenue to Uncle Sam and to other political subdivisions which depend on income taxes would be enormous and, politically, such a change in tax policy would be unpopular, particularly if the revenue gap were filled by imposing some other type of tax.

There is some possibility that there will be a resurrection of lower rates for long-term capital gains. But, as mentioned, this is far from a certainty.

While investors should figure tax codifications into their decision making, avoiding taxes should not be an ultimate goal; making money should be that goal, albeit saving taxes is part of the decision-making process.

Even if capital gains continue to be taxed at ordinary income rates, there is still an advantage of capital appreciation versus current income. That is, investors can control the time when they realize capital gains, either deferring them or realizing them at the proper time.

But one thing is clear. Holding a poor investment just because its sale would incur a tax is sheer folly. I would prefer to pay more in taxes than forego better results from investments, and most thinking people would agree.

Not really in the realm of money management, per se, but relevant to budgeting and planning overall, are some of the financial planning devices such as gifting to others shares of appreciated stock if the recipients could then sell such stock and pay lower tax rates. Of course, charitable giving of appreciated assets instead of cash or the creation of charitable remainder trusts, thereby acquiring both charitable gift deductions and increased income, are perfectly legal and desirable ways to mitigate potential tax liabilities.

Accountants, lawyers, and financial planners of all kinds can advise on these subjects, and although they have little to do with decision making on specific investment issues, they can dramatically impact investment results. Investors are well advised to review these and other similar subjects with professional advisors who closely follow the changing tax laws and regulations. Avoiding such consultation can prove costly.

A CASE IN POINT

Several years ago, a man who was worth well over $100 million approached me and requested that I assist him in planning for his future. He indicated that he had no financial problems, per se, except that he wanted to ensure that he did not incur some liability that would cause him to forfeit those assets. As it turned out, this man had never been married, had no children, had no intention of being married and, upon death, was going to leave everything he had accumulated to his church.

And so I told him that I didn't know how to protect him from every kind of liability that he might encounter. However, I gave him one suggestion, which was to take a portion of that money and create a charitable remainder trust. He would place the assets into a trust, from which he would receive income for the rest of his life, but upon death the assets would revert to his church. This would accomplish just about what he was trying to accomplish in the first place, with the added benefit of some tax advantages.

He found my suggestion much to his liking, and promised to speak with his attorney the same week about a possible course of action. That was the end of our interview. A week later I had still not heard from him so I called to see if he had spoken with his attorney. He replied, "I talked to my attorney and I've done it." I asked, "*What* have you done?" And he said, "Well, you told me to take some of my assets and create a charitable trust, but I've decided, the heck with it, I'm going to put *everything* in that trust."

And I said, "Do you mean to tell me that you have created a trust, and you put *all* of your assets into the trust?" And he said, "Yes, my attorney objected, but I said '*Do it.*' So the attorney has drawn the agreement."

Flabbergasted, I asked, "Well, did you name my trust company as trustee?" And he said, "Oh, no. I have three friends in different parts of the country, whom I have named as co-trustees." Stunned by this new revelation, I pressed him for more answers. "Do you mean to tell me that you have turned over everything you have to three people who live in three different parts of the country, and they, from this point on, are going to be managing your money for you?" And he said, "That's right."

"What did you do with your tax shelter assets that you had?" I asked. I recalled that he had a lot of real estate on which he had tax shelter investments. He replied "I have placed everything in there." And I said, "So you have lost all of the tax benefits of those assets?" And he said, "Well, I never thought of that."

"Well," I said, "I think you had better think about it, and I think you had better call your lawyer and rescind that trust." Which, in fact he did.

But this story illustrates that even a very wealth person might fail to think about the consequences of hasty decisions. People tend to take as gospel what they hear, without giving thought to what they're doing. While my advice was good, he carried it to an extreme, which could have been disastrous for him in many different ways.

People should give a great deal of thought to what they do; just because somebody advises them to do something doesn't necessarily mean that only one alternative exists.

CONCLUSION

The best advice that can be given to investors is that they should manage assets with a goal toward making money. Managing tax consequences should be only part of their total strategy, not a "be all and end all" in itself.

One other thought about the capital gains tax is important to investors. Uncle Sam's capital gains tax can also be labeled his capital loss tax. If taxable investors have, in fact, capital losses, realization of such losses can be valuable. After all, under current tax laws, a loss (be it long-term or short-term) is first an offset to realized gains and then an offset against income itself. Admittedly, the annual deductibility of net losses is limited, but the unused net losses can be carried over for future years. Consequently, the establishment of a loss on an asset, unpleasant though it might be, can become an annuity benefit provided by Uncle Sam.

Many who own securities with an unrealized loss, but who continue to have faith in the future of those securities, might well be advised to double up on their holdings, wait 31 days, and then sell the original holdings. This is a way of establishing a loss but maintaining good, long-term assets. Of course, there are associated risks, such as the market value 31 days later, and the commission costs of required transactions, but it is a perfectly legitimate way to save taxes and enhance current income.

Finally, one further aspect of capital gains is noteworthy. Under current tax laws, capital gains are forgiven at death. Assets held at death acquire the cost basis of the market value at death for the investors' heirs. This "stepped up basis" for assets is still a loophole in the tax system. How long it will remain is a matter of speculation. Eliminating it has long been a platform of many congressmen charged with tax legislation, but for now it remains.

the instruments

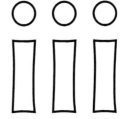

chapter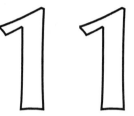

equities

Of course, selection of individual stocks for an investment portfolio is vitally important to the ultimate success of the portfolio in reaching its goals. Many investors consider security analysis an occult enterprise, but it is not. More often than not, stock selection depends on common sense.

Industries and individual companies within industries have characters of their own. Yet, in the final analysis, there are only a few different kinds of stocks, as listed below:

- Long-term growth companies

- Cyclical companies

- Interest rate sensitive companies

- Emerging growth companies

- Special situation companies

- The "mundane"

LONG-TERM GROWTH COMPANIES

Without question, the core or emphasis of any well constructed stock portfolio should include the acquisition and holding of company stocks which promise potential in long-term earnings growth. Such stocks are hardly ever inexpensive relative to the market itself, but they offer the best opportunity for increased value over any reasonable period of time.

Why? Because these companies are in the fastest growing industries in our economy. These are companies whose sales and earnings have grown and can be expected to grow at an above average rate because their products and services are experiencing increased demand from consumers.

It is not really very difficult to define which industries and which companies comprise this category. Among them are the following:

- Ethical Drug Companies

- Hospital Supply and Management Companies

- Electrical Equipment and Electronic Companies

- Information Processing Companies

- Pollution Control Companies

- Telecommunication Companies

- Others

The so-called "graying of America," the demographic trend toward not only an expanding number of senior citizens but people living longer lives, has been a boon to businesses operating in the health care field. Major ethical drug companies are constantly engaged in major research efforts to develop new drugs to meet increasing demands for treating diseases of all kinds, not only those suffered by the elderly, but those prevalent throughout the entire population.

Companies such as Merck, Lilly, Pfizer, Bristol Myers Squibb—to mention a few—have been very successful over the years in such endeavors, and as a result, both sales and profits have soared. Although, from time to time, investors have worried about such things as price controls on drugs, these companies have prospered and should continue to prosper as not only the volume of their sales increases but as the cost of production of their products declines. Moreover, these companies are not subject to economic cycles, as are companies in other sectors. The use of drugs to combat disease is a necessity (far cheaper, for instance, than surgical procedures), in good times and bad.

The same premise applies to Hospital Management and Hospital Supply companies. To some extent, they are more cyclical than drug companies because of various factors. Hospitals may, from time to time, experience decreased use of beds due to hospital over-building in different geographic areas or lack of such procedures as "elective surgery" in poor economic times, and so on. And hospital suppliers may periodically suffer from declining sales to hospitals and other sources for sales. But, in the long run, there is almost no end to the growth of the hospital and medical supply business, both disposable supplies and equipment. Companies such as Abbott Labs, Baxter International, Johnson & Johnson, and others should enjoy enhanced earnings for the foreseeable future.

There is no question that ours is the age of advancing technology, and increased use of electrical equipment and electronics is a foregone conclusion. The behemoth in these industries is probably the bluest chip of them all, General Electric. A highly diversified company, GE can be described as a veritable mutual fund of technology. It has always been an efficiently managed company, is strongly financed, and is already a major factor in almost all important areas of scientific research and development as well as being a large manufacturer and provider of equipment and systems. It operates world-wide and is a company whose stock should be held in virtually all stock portfolios.

Other quality stocks of above average growth would include Amp, Intel, and Motorola, to name only a few. As an aside, Motorola commands special attention. Not only is it the leading domestic manufacturer and supplier of semiconductors, it is also a dominant factor in the fast growing cellular telephone business. Those companies which directly market cellular phones have become very competitive; some will survive and grow, others may die, but chances are strong that Motorola will remain the leading manufacturer of such equipment. This is the stuff of which long-term sales and earnings growth is made.

Contrary to some pundits, the computer is not dead. In fact, computer usage could be said to remain in a strong growth mode, and companies which make computers and service or sell them remain among the leading growth companies of America. In recent years, I.B.M. has lost market share to the competition, but it is still the leader and innovator in the mainframe business. Companies such as Hewlett Packard, Automatic Data, and others should be among those considered in any growth stock list.

One of the potentially exciting areas of investment opportunity is pollution control. Generally speaking, environmental control and improvement has become almost a mandate of the people. Not only will government continue to spend heavily in the areas of air and water purification and waste disposal, but so too will private industry, and this offers opportunity to companies engaged in this field. Again, there is a long list of such companies, but an obvious and outstanding leader in the field is Waste Management.

Telecommunications equipment and service is another dynamic area of growth, and it embraces a long list of specific equipment and service. As mentioned above, the cellular phone is one of them, but not to be overlooked are the providers of other equipment and services. While there is a long list of large and small companies in this industry, there is one very obvious quality company called AT&T. For years many considered this company dull and unprogressive. But it is now emerging as one of the quality growth companies of the world, having become unshackled from regulation, and comprising a combination of superior research capability as well as outstanding manufacturing capacity. Not many have called AT&T a great growth company, but it has become just that.

An area of interest for future growth is, obviously, the rebuilding of the infrastructure. More and more demands are compelling federal, state, and local governments to build new roads, improve water and sewer systems, replace obsolete bridges, and so on. While such construction activity has not been included in lists of growth industries in the past, public policy is focusing increasing attention on it, and there will be continued growth in this area not only in the U.S. but in other parts of the world, such as the Middle East, Eastern Europe, and Russia. Companies such as Caterpillar Corp. (the leading supplier of earth moving equipment), Fluor Corp., and Morris Knudsen (engineering and construction companies) could be big beneficiaries of the growth in this area. Investors should not overlook the obvious: public construction of all kinds is a way of providing work for the unemployed masses of the U.S. and other nations, particularly those with limited skills and training. This may be one of the fastest growing sectors of the economy of this and other nations for many years to come as, hopefully, spending on defense will moderate and governments can begin to direct additional funds to their respective domestic scenes.

In addition to the growth areas enumerated above, there are certainly growth companies in industries that are not necessarily growth industries per se.

Such an example can be found in the food sector. Consumption of food itself is not really in a growth mode, except as the population continues to increase. But, in recent years, new trends have emerged in food consumption. The trend toward two people in a family working is a relatively new social more for the American people. A strong beneficiary of this trend has been the fast food and restaurant business, with McDonalds as the prime example. The undisputed leader and innovator in the fast food business, this company has expanded and prospered, and can be expected to continue this trend into the next century. In the restaurant business, and catering to the family, General Mills has performed an outstanding job in creating chains of Red Lobster and Olive Garden restaurants. Certainly, these companies should be included as growth companies.

Other examples are companies that have taken a share of the market in the merchandising industry. The success of, say, Gap. Inc., Home Depot, The Limited, Wal-Mart Stores, Nike, Tandy, and others is directly related to the ability of these companies to give the public what it wants and needs, at a reasonable cost and with convenience. Not all of these companies will remain in a growth mode (fashion could change, stiff competition could occur, etc.), but investors can profit by observing consumer attitudes and companies that are meeting consumer demands.

A list of quality growth companies whose stock can be held by long-term investors with a high heart could go on and on. Although I should not belabor the matter, among specialty companies that fit a special need could be Boeing, Coca-Cola, International Flavors & Fragrances, Pioneer Hi Bred, Procter & Gamble, General Re, and others. The main point that I make is that growth companies do not necessarily have to be companies in the "glamour" growth industries. They can be companies that have a special niche in their own industries or that offer products or services in some special, demand-providing way.

CYCLICAL COMPANIES

There is a long list of industries and companies which are cyclical in nature. That is, they benefit or suffer from economic conditions as they prevail from time to time. Investors can make money by investing in the stocks of such companies, but they must be aware that proper timing of purchase and sale of these stocks is vital for success.

A good case in point is the automobile industry. It is one of the largest industries in this country—and the world—if one considers all of the businesses allied to automobiles. In this country, of course, General Motors, Ford, and Chrysler dominate this field.

It is almost axiomatic to say that the time to buy automobile stocks is when these companies are having a difficult time. This was the case during the 1973-1974 recession; it happened again in 1981 and still again in 1991, when the recession brought havoc to the automobile industry. Sales and profits plummeted during those times. As a matter of fact, there was a period during the 1970s when General Motors operated at a deficit, Ford was rumored to be bankrupt, and every one "knew" that Chrysler was going out of business. That was an ideal time to buy the stocks. Patient investors doubled and tripled their investment, some doing even better than that in the ensuing years; it took patience and fortitude, but the patience paid off.

The real trick to making money from these stocks is also to sell them at the right time. And when is that? It is when everything is going well for the industry, sales are up, dividends are rising, and stock splits are occurring. In short, the time to buy these stocks is when no one wants them, and the time to sell them is when everyone else is buying because the stocks still look cheap. John Templeton is a strong proponent of this strategy, and he is willing to wait three or four years before realizing the reward.

This kind of contrary investing can be very profitable, as far as cyclical companies are concerned. Contrarianism does not require much insight, but it does require recognition of the fact that stocks of some companies trade on a predictable cyclical pattern, the timing of which is difficult to pinpoint successfully. Indeed, in the case of the cyclicals, the "hit'em where they're not" philosophy can work for patient investors.

I am mindful of the answer Baron Rothschild gave in response to the question of how to be a successful investor. He said the secret of successful investing is to be "as nice a person as you can." What he meant was that a successful investor is one who is accommodating to others. "When other people want to sell, buy; when other people want to buy, sell; you will always be buying low and selling high."

In reality, Baron Rothschild was not all that altruistic. He actually rigged markets and brainwashed investors into establishing positions in certain markets in order that he might take advantage of them. But, at least in theory, being a "good guy" can produce good profits through judicious trading in cyclical stocks.

There are many other cyclical stocks, which require accurate timing in their purchase and sale. For most investors—including myself—this is a very arduous task. Therefore, for the most part, I avoid the cyclicals except upon rare occasion. Among the industries which I include as cyclical are:

- Air Transport
- Automobile

– Chemical

– Housing

– Railroad

– Real Estate

– Steel

– Textile

– Trucking

Although there are some very fine, well managed and strongly financed companies in these industries, I recommend that most investors shy away from them. Money can be made by nimble trading, but I prefer to leave to others the task of capitalizing on cyclical stocks.

INTEREST RATE SENSITIVE COMPANIES

Not exactly cyclical companies, interest rate sensitive companies are those whose profits are affected adversely by high interest rates and positively by low interest rates. They are companies whose stocks rise in value when interest rates decline, and fall when interest rates rise, and are found in the following industries:

– Banking and Finance

– Insurance

– Savings and Loans

– Utilities

To determine when to buy and/or sell these stocks, investors must be equipped with a fundamental perspective about the outlook for interest rates, which is not quite so easy as most people think.

The real determinant of the outlook for interest rates is the trend in inflation. If the cost of living (or Consumer Price Index) can be expected to rise at a precipitous rate, so too can interest rates. It makes sense that higher costs for money adversely affect industries which are heavy buyers of money.

Banks are a good example. They make money by borrowing from their depositors at one rate and selling to their borrowers at a higher rate. The spread between what money costs them (plus, of course, operating expenses) and what they receive for it comprises the profits of banks. Of course, this is an over simplification, but it is the basic strategy banks employ to make money.

Unfortunately, when the cost of money increases (rates on savings accounts, certificates of deposit, etc.), banks are not able to offset this entirely by increasing rates to borrowers. Either the banks are locked into loan rates (i.e., mortgages), or higher rates discourage borrowing itself, and so bank earnings are hurt. When the opposite occurs, banks prosper.

Other financial institutions have similar problems, with only slight variations; it suffices to say that much of their investments are locked in at fixed rates, and when money becomes more expensive, profits suffer.

Again, investors can make money in financial stocks, but they should recognize cyclical swings in earnings (and, therefore, stock prices) relative to whatever happens in the money markets.

The story is slightly different for utility stocks, and rather than discuss them here, I devote a special chapter to the subject.

EMERGING GROWTH COMPANIES

Most of the recognized blue chip growth companies were once emerging growth companies. The term "emerging growth company" really means a relatively small company which is either developing a new product or service, or is engaged in a business which, although small at the present time, will become a major enterprise.

It is through investing in emerging growth companies that fortunes have been made, but it is equally true that such investment can lead to massive losses.

It is self-evident that if an investor can discern a company which either has developed or is on the verge of developing "a better mouse trap," he should buy some of that stock. The rewards can be enormous.

I recall, for example, buying the stock of a company named Haloid Corporation. Frankly, at the time, I was not completely sure what the company actually produced, but I knew it was involved in some esoteric research of momentous proportion. The rest was history. Haloid eventually changed its name to Xerox. It had completely revolutionized the business of making copies, and investors reaped enormous benefits.

There are many other similar examples, but for every success story there are literally hundreds of similar companies which went out of business for one reason or another. Finances were lacking, there was strong competition, experts in research were not good managers of operating companies, and products or services were not very good or in demand after all.

One specific example I remember was a company called Transitron. The stock was sold publicly many years ago on the premise that the principals of the company were the preeminent experts on transistors and how to make them. Investors rushed to buy the stock. Within months, the company was virtually bankrupt. Why? It was simply because Texas Instruments, Motorola, and others had better products at lower prices. What people thought was going to be the leader in an obvious growth industry became a virtual bankruptcy instead.

Today, there is an obvious emerging growth industry. It is called biotechnology. The science of genetic transfer and the development of interferon devices for all sorts of purposes, including human health and, particularly (and hopefully), for finding a cure for cancer, represents a tremendous breakthrough. Companies such as Amgen, Genentech, and Immunex have already announced developments of great magnitude. This is exciting, and the science is only in its infancy. But who knows which company will discover what, when, and for what purpose? Even given successful development, can the products, devices, and systems be implemented? If so, for what profit? Furthermore, is it possible that whatever is developed will soon be outdated by something else? Perhaps one or two companies in this new field will emerge as real winners. Or, perhaps one of the large ethical drug companies will be the eventual producer in biotechnology. But there is a long list of participants in biotechnology, not all of which are publicly held companies. And to pick the one or two stocks *today*, which will emerge tomorrow, is fraught with peril.

Obviously, other companies exist in other industries which are small, but which by the end of this decade will be household names. Perhaps they are engaged in health care, maybe in the operation of public facilities or in various consumer services, but selecting them is not easy.

For investors who are unable or unwilling to devote the time and effort to ferret out such opportunities, there are some emerging growth company mutual funds, and investors should consider buying a few shares of those funds or, at least, looking at the individual holdings of those funds for clues about which companies exist which professional investment managers consider good, emerging companies.

For me (and for most investors) I leave the investment in emerging growth companies to others, along with the thought that I wish them every success and, most importantly, a good deal of luck.

SPECIAL SITUATION COMPANIES

There is hardly any precise description of what is called a "special situation company." The reason is that it is just that, a company whose stock looks like an interesting purchase for "some special situation."

And this can run the gamut from a "buy out" play, a company in bankruptcy which may re-emerge, and a company which has a special "asset play," to a company that is changing management or ownership, a company that might be about to receive a windfall, or almost any other situation imaginable.

Certainly, special situations have to be analyzed individually, and there really is not much advice to offer to investors about how to invest in them.

Therefore, it suffices to say that from time to time opportunities do evolve in which investors can make money, and their eyes and ears should constantly be open for such an eventuality. But a strong word of warning is in order. Hot tips about which stock is going to do what, because of what, are fraught with peril. Just because someone says so, writes so, or thinks so, it will not necessarily be so. And if it does, it may not be in the form that the beholder envisions. If information truly comes from the inside of a company, it may be illegal and, as a matter of fact, "insiders" do not always know what they purport to know.

However, one trend that is developing is intriguing. Many companies which were bought out or leveraged (borrowing the purchase funds) have started to resell stock in the public marketplace (RJR Nabisco, Duracell, and others were examples in 1991). This raising of equity capital to reduce debt may in itself result in better profits for the companies, and such companies, on this basis, may become interesting speculation plays.

There is another trend, worthy of mention, that may develop over the months and years ahead.

Mergers are not dead, and many will occur over the next several years. But instead of being "buy outs" for cash, as experienced during the 1980s, they may be on the basis of exchange of stock from the acquiring company to shareholders of the acquired. This could lead to a rerun of the experience of the 1960s, and if so, could result in a windfall for the stockholders of the "gobblor" rather than of the "gobblee."

I recall when Litton Industries was a major acquiror of other companies. Litton stock sold at a high price/earnings ratio, and the company would exchange its stock for the stock of companies it was buying, which had higher earnings per share than Litton. Sure, the stockholders of the acquired company received a "proper profit," but Litton acquired higher earnings. And the stock market would "celebrate" by pushing Litton stock even higher on the theory that this was justified because of automatically increased profits. It was not exactly a "Ponzi Scheme," but it was a pyramid scheme that eventually broke. In the meantime, Litton stockholders made money.

This may be one type of "special situation" which will occur, and investors would be well advised to watch for it.

THE MUNDANE

When all is said and done, a large bulk of stocks available in the market are mundane or average. They are the stocks of major industries and major companies, as well as minor ones. Among the industries which I consider mundane are:

- Merchandizing

- Oil

- Food, beverage, and tobacco

- Other consumer good and services

By the term, "mundane," I do not imply uninteresting, nor do I mean industries that investors should avoid. I use the term mundane to denote stocks of companies which will do well through thick and thin, which, longer term, will perform about in line with the market, and which are neither dynamic on the upside nor highly speculative on the downside.

A well diversified portfolio should probably include some stocks of a relatively mundane nature. And, as a matter of fact, there are times when these stocks can have dramatic turns in price, either up or down.

Witness the dramatic moves in oil stocks during the last couple of decades. Traumatic events including the oil embargo of 1973, a run up in oil prices in 1980 and, again, in the summer of 1990, the Iraqi invasion of Kuwait all precipitated fears of oil shortages throughout the world. But shortages in anything relative to demand bring about price increases, and price increases in oil spur higher profits for oil companies and, therefore, higher prices for their stocks. In fact, this phenomenon is somewhat illusory because those higher profits are really *inventory*, not operating profits. Every time oil profits have risen because of higher oil prices, capital expenses for development of new sources of oil have shot up commensurately. The result has been better reported earnings on the income statements but deterioration of capital budgets. Nevertheless, oil stock prices in recent years have gone way up and way down depending on the price of oil.

Most stock observers would agree that the oil business is not really a secular growth business, or at least, the oil sector is not growing much more than the economy as a whole. In fact, there are major strides in the direction of developing alternate sources of fuel for energy. Coal, natural gas, nuclear power, even solar power are among the alternate sources. Consequently, an industry which has come to the fore during the age of the combustion engine, is now becoming one that participates in the economy but does not exceed it.

Of course, investors can expect that there will be periods when international events will favorably or negatively affect oil companies and their stocks. Investors should be aware of this and take advantage of these events when they occur. But in the meantime, oil stocks should sell at about a market average, yield a market return on dividends, and buyers of such stocks should recognize them as mundane.

There may be one major exception to this observation. I regard oil drilling companies such as Schlumberger and Halliburton as good growth companies. To avoid oil shortages in the future, there is little question that drilling activity will have to increase throughout the world, and these specialty companies are well positioned not only to assist oil companies in exploration and development but also to work with governments around the world to improve drilling results. Far from mundane, the oil service companies are rightly categorized as long-term growth companies.

There is no sense belaboring the obvious and commenting to a great extent on other mundane areas. Obviously, there are individual companies within mundane industries which merit aggressive long-term investing. I have already highlighted some of these. To mention just a few other notable areas: merchandizing, food, beverage, tobacco, and other consumer goods and service companies experience changing fortunes from time to time. However, why the average investor should be excited about them for the longer term defies the imagination.

chapter 12

utility stocks

The single biggest holdings of individual and institutional investors is in stock of companies in the utility industry. In fact, the market value of utility stocks in the marketplace is a staggering 15 percent of the market value of all stocks.

Utility stocks are very popular with investors in search of reasonable rates of return from dividends, as well as stable and predictable results.

I have always regarded utility stocks as substitutes for bonds rather than true stocks. And whether or not they admit this, utility stockholders usually view these instruments in a similar fashion.

Thirty or forty years ago, investors often thought of utility stocks as growth stocks, and for good reason. Enormous increases in energy consumption occurred along with the advent of more and more electrical and electronic devices; innovations such as air conditioning revolutionized not only the way people lived and worked, but where they lived. However, it is apparent that the great growth in the utility business is past, not prologue. For sure, some growth remains because of increased usage. But utility companies are no longer growth entities, at least relative to the economy itself or to other industries.

And utility stock prices reflect this truth. As a matter of fact, utility investors pay much more attention to dividends than to earnings as such, and so the selection of such stocks should have, and does have, a different focus than the selection of other stocks.

Prices of utility stocks are extremely "interest rate sensitive." Because utility stocks are "competitors" of bonds for investors seeking income, they trade in the marketplace on a direct comparison with bonds and, therefore, in correlation with interest rates as they vary over time.

The big advantage of utility stocks versus bonds is that utilities experience a fairly predictable increase in their dividends, while bonds pay a fixed rate of return. As a result, utility stocks provide an inflation hedge for the income investor, whereas bonds do not.

There are other advantages of utility stocks over bonds. For example, in periods of declining interest rates, utility stock prices rise in value, but they are not called away or redeemed, as are many bonds. Consequently, an investor enjoys capital appreciation at the same time as his income is held intact. In a sense, quality utility stocks can be said to be perpetual maturity bonds with variable income, with such income almost always increasing. If this sounds like the best of all possible worlds, in a sense, it is.

But the nature of utility stocks also raises a red flag. Their stock prices can be volatile. Whereas in declining interest rate periods utility stock prices rise more than do bond prices, so too in rising interest rate periods utility stock prices decline more than bonds because they are not protected by a maturity date. Herein lies the risk of utility stocks in general.

Of course, there are some other risks. The utility industry is heavily regulated both in the services it must provide consumers and in the rates it can charge. Attitudes of various regulatory commissions on these subjects vary considerably, with some commissions very "consumer conscious" and others recognizing the necessity for utility companies to earn high rates of return in order to finance necessary capital expense.

The Three Mile Island "disaster" a few years ago was much more of a disaster than is generally recognized. Certainly, the malfunctioning of a major nuclear power facility with all of the attendant problems was a very untoward event. But an even larger result of that event was both a curtailment of nuclear power plant construction and an enormous increase in the capital costs for such plants due to environmental safeguards mandated by the experience of Three Mile Island.

Many electric utility companies have been forced to either abandon nuclear power production facilities altogether, or to incur much higher costs for maintaining them. And in many cases, these utilities have not been allowed to increase rates commensurate with these staggering capital costs. The stocks of such utility companies have suffered in the market and some of the companies have had to reduce or eliminate dividends as investors found that the stocks were not the safe, predictable, dividend-paying investments that they had been led to believe.

In recent years, many utility companies have experienced a healthy increase in their cash flow, not only from earnings but also through cash flow from depreciation and other sources. Since many utilities have sufficient generating capacity from power plants already in place, or from new technology providing the ability to buy power from others in times of peak demand, that cash flow has not been required to finance new facilities. As a result, utility companies have increased dividends and invested cash in diversified activities, hoping to provide better earnings growth.

Unfortunately, however, not all of these diversified activities have paid off. Witness the tremendous losses of Florida Power and Light (F.P.L. Group) in its venture into the insurance business, and the horrendous problem of Arizona Public Service as a result of investments in the savings and loan industry.

Although the electric utility industry is a stable one, a predictable one, and therefore, a good place for conservative investors to place capital, it is not without problems, requiring careful scrutiny of such stocks.

Following are some of the criteria I use and suggest for the selection of electric utility stocks:

- Hold stocks only of utility companies operating in high population growth areas (for instance, the South and the Southeast).

- Hold stocks only of companies enjoying favorable regulatory attitudes (Wisconsin, for example).

- Hold stocks of companies which have ample generating capacity for the foreseeable future (there are many).

- Avoid stocks of companies having problems with unfinished nuclear power plants.

- Most important, hold stocks of companies which have a proven record and a stated policy of regularly increasing dividends, preferably every year.

This latter criterion is most important. As a matter of fact, it is even more important than the yield or rate of return currently available from a utility stock. The main thrust of what utility stock investors should seek is increased dividends on an annual basis. And there is a simple statistical exercise investors can use to measure whether a utility has the ability to raise its dividends.

It is not difficult to extract from the income statement of a utility (or from, say, a Standard & Poor statistical sheet on the company), the net earnings as reported in dollars. Adding to the net earnings a portion of the reported depreciation charge (one-half of it is reasonable), and subtracting from this the so-called "interest due to construction" (a short-term, non-recurring phenomenon) gives an investor a conservative estimate of the net cash available to pay dividends. Dividing this net cash by the number of outstanding shares of the company provides the amount of cash per share which the company can pay.

If the current dividend which the utility pays is no more than 60 percent of the available cash flow, then there is room for future dividend increases. But if the current dividend is 80 to 90 percent of that figure, chances are slim for much of an increase.

This "rule of thumb" approach is not without variables and certainly is not foolproof, but it does help eliminate problem companies and focus on the thriving utilities.

There is a long list of electric utility companies which meet these criteria. It makes little sense to try to list all of them, but among the better situated utility companies are Duke Power, Teco Energy, Wisconsin Energy, and Central & South West.

One final thought about electric utility stocks is noteworthy. From time to time utility stock prices move to levels which are not competitive to bond prices. Income investors should compare the rate of return from both. Then, when utility dividends *plus* projected increases in dividends over a five-year period do not equal yields available from high grade, ten- to fifteen-year maturity call protected corporate bonds, utility stocks should be avoided in favor of bonds. After all, provision of income (which can be spent or reinvested) is the main reason for such investments, and when that purpose is negated, considering the downside risk of utility stock prices versus bond prices, investors should make substantive changes in their portfolios in favor of bonds.

TELEPHONE UTILITIES

Electric utilities are not the only types of utilities; many investors prefer telephone utility stocks, and for some very good reasons.

The telephone utility industry is growing and should expand at a faster rate than the electric industry. Therefore, there is more opportunity for both capital appreciation and dividend increase in this sector.

The breakup of "Ma Bell" has created several well financed, superbly managed, and fast growing operating telephone companies available to the public for stock investment. Investors should not overlook the so-called "Baby Bells," or those companies "spun out" of the breakup of AT&T, which offer good potential for income and, as a matter of fact, have shown an ability to "grow" earnings and dividends at an average to above average rate.

Without going into detail about this industry, I believe that conservative investors can hold such stocks in much the way they hold electric utility stocks. There is scant difference between the outlook for one company versus another, but standing by the thesis which emphasizes companies operating in population growth areas, one conclusion could be that Bell South will emerge as the "pick of the litter" for the longer term.

chapter 13

bonds

Contrary to all of the discussion about stocks, there is, without question, a place in investment portfolios for bonds. But investors should recognize bonds for exactly what they are. They are debt of an issuer, be it Uncle Sam who sells U.S. Treasury Bonds, be it corporations which borrow money through the issuance of bonds, or be it States, Municipalities or other political subdivisions which sell bonds in the marketplace. The investor in a bond is, in effect, renting his money to the issuer for a rate of return.

Rates of return can vary considerably over time; those who recall rates available from bonds only over the last few years have either short memories or a lack of knowledge of history.

For example, during World War II, the U.S had so-called "pegged money" rates. Conducting war was expensive, and in order to keep its borrowing cost low, the federal government, through the monetization policies of the Federal Reserve System, kept interest rates low—very low—and offset the possibility of rampant inflation by imposing strict wage and price controls as well as high tax rates, all with the purported purpose of limiting profiteering from the defense effort.

It was not uncommon for U.S. Treasury Bonds to yield 1 1/2 to 2 percent and, in fact, long-term U.S. Treasury Bonds—nicknamed the "Vics," for Victory Bonds—maturing in 1972, carried an interest rate of 2 1/2 percent.

Abnormally low rates persisted into the 1950s. During that decade, as a matter of fact, I recall that every three months, the U.S. Treasury would issue 1 1/2 percent five-year notes which banks and other investors purchased in large quantities for the humorous reason that after holding them for one year, the government would exchange those notes for 2 3/4 percent bonds due in 1980, a seemingly "glorious" return at that time.

During the Eisenhower Administration, there was a hue and cry in Congress over the fact that the Secretary of the Treasury, a Mr. Humphrey, had the audacity to issue 30-year maturity 3 1/4 percent bonds, thereby "mortgaging the future of Americans" at an "enormous" rate of interest. There was, in fact, a movement afoot in Congress to impeach Mr. Humphrey for his "treasonous" act. By hindsight we now realize that what Mr. Humphrey actually did was to borrow money at no cost at all. Uncle Sam received 1953 dollars while paying a rate which, over the 30-year life of the bonds, was less than the average inflation rate of that period. And, of course, in addition, the bondholders were taxed by Uncle Sam for the interest they earned.

It was not really until the 1960s that interest rates began to rise but, even then, nowhere to the extent we have experienced in recent years. During the early 1960s, long-term U.S. Treasury bonds yielded about 4 percent and corporate bonds about 4 1/2 percent. Then rates began to explode. The outbreak of the Vietnam War and a policy of "guns and butter" emanating from Washington triggered inflation and started a rash of bond offerings from both government and private industry to finance both the war and domestic economic expansion. This interest rate and inflation explosion was temporarily aborted by wage and price controls in effect between 1971 and 1974. But interest rates rose again at the end of the 1970s and early 1980s, as both inflation and interest rates went to double digit levels (10 percent and higher).

For most of the 1980s, interest rates declined, as did inflation. But as we enter the 1990s, interest rates remain high on an historical basis.

Will rates recede to the low levels of yesteryear? Probably not. Uncle Sam has been, and will continue to be, a net borrower of large amounts of money to finance the national deficit, thus competing with the private sector, which will always possess a formidable demand for capital.

But those who believe that high interest rates will remain a permanent fixture of the economic landscape are ignoring what has happened in the past. The critical determinant of where interest rates head, both short- and long-term, will be whatever happens on the inflation front.

An inflation rate of roughly 4 percent, with a slight variance from time to time, will prevail throughout the 1990s. Given that this is the case, a "normal" rate for long-term U.S. Treasury Bonds should be somewhere between 7 and 7 1/2 percent. From here, it follows that "normal" rates on high grade corporate bonds should be about 8 to 8 1/2 percent, and normalized rates for longer term tax-exempt bonds should stand at approximately 5 1/2 percent. These are rates that bond investors, those who "rent" their money, should expect.

If this turns out to be correct, then bond investors will enjoy a negative rate of return on their capital if they spend the income, because the purchasing power of their capital will erode regardless of the prevailing inflation rate.

This is why I am not enamored of bonds as a way to invest money over any long time frame, except as a way to receive a cash flow either for reinvestment purposes or for living costs.

Nevertheless, I am also aware that many investors need this cash flow, and that bonds—particularly high-grade bonds—provide such a flow without the risk of nominal loss of capital.

To the extent that investors *do* buy and hold bonds, I make the following suggestions:

- Own only high-grade bonds (U.S. Treasury, Corporate, or Tax Exempt).

- In times when rates are above the norm, hold bonds with longer term maturities and *with call protection.*

- Know that bonds, like stocks, should be managed.

Concerning bond quality, most investors should pay heed to the research of rating services (Standard & Poor, Moody's, etc.) and avoid anything rated less than A by the services. In recent years, investors have been badly burned by stretching into lower grade bonds, those in risk of default, or those issued by entities with less than good balance sheets or sources of funds with which to pay interest or capital at maturity. Such investors have been lulled by high rates, but they have found what is always true, that one gets what one buys, and junk is often what it claims to be—junk.

About maturities, many people invest in short-term instruments because they view such investments as "safer," and "more liquid." But those opting for shorter term maturities run a real risk of experiencing lower interest rates and, therefore, lower income as their short-term investments mature. If an investor rents money for a rate of return, he should at least desire continuity of that return.

Concerning bond management, there are all sorts of techniques which investors should employ, depending upon what has happened in the marketplace and what can be foreseen to occur. For instance, as interest rates rise, maturities should be lengthened; as they go down, maturities of holdings should either be shortened or, perhaps, held steady. Such devices as adopting a "ladder approach" whereby an investor holds bonds of various maturities and is, therefore, cushioned against adverse bond price movements, or holding so-called "cushion bonds" (bonds selling at a premium over redemption value) can help obviate severe losses in times of rising rates.

Personally, most of the time (particularly in the taxable bond market) I am enamored of bonds selling at a discount to face value. By that I mean bonds available in the market paying slightly less than the going rate but promising some capital gain at maturity. Investors can thus purchase bonds that yield reasonable rates of return and also promise protection against premature redemption as well as capital gain.

On the other hand, I am less enamored of so-called "zero coupon" bonds, meaning bonds bought at a deep discount by paying no interest. These bonds often appear to be "cheap," but I like assets which direct cash flow to me and give me flexibility to do with such funds as I see fit, either spending or reinvesting them. Certainly, zero coupon bonds make no sense for those who depend on interest income to offset living costs.

The securities industry has issued a plethora of shares of bond funds in recent years. These are mutual funds or investment trusts that invest in bonds, running the gamut from U.S. Treasury Bonds and corporate bonds, to tax-exempt bonds and junk bonds.

My recommendation is that they too should be avoided. Many bond funds are invested but not actively managed. Like stock mutual funds, they are almost always over diversified, and one of the most insidious parts of many such funds is that they pay "return of capital dividends" which are illusory because they are not dividends at all but return of capital. Such dividends usually are high during low interest rate periods and low as interest rates rise. In effect, then, investors get their money back at just the wrong time.

Investors should know that bond prices rise or fall in direct relation to interest rate movements. It is not all bad news if a bond price declines. This means that interest rates have gone up. It also means that there is an opportunity to establish tax losses by selling such bonds and buying others while, at the same time, increasing income.

In summary, although I am skeptical that bonds provide the best investment for making money, I realize that they may make sense for many investors, and for many diverse reasons. However, prudence and active management in bond investing can produce greater results than owning them passively.

chapter

cash reserves

"How much of my money should be invested in the stock market?"

This is probably the single question investors ask most often. For the truly long-term, total return, compounding of income type investor, the answer almost always is "most of it." But the real answer to that question depends on more basic questions surrounding the purposes and goals of the investor.

To the extent that an investor has a short-term need for capital, it makes good sense to keep such funds liquid and free from the short-term price fluctuations of longer term investments. Though this goes without saying, many investors fall into the trap of trying to maximize results over the short term, often falling victim to unexpected or unforeseen aberrations in the market brought on by traumatic events.

A perfect example of this occurred during the summer of 1990 when Iraq invaded Kuwait, raising the specter of a further incursion into Saudi Arabia and the possibility of a major disruption of the world's oil supply. Looming was a potentially disastrous economic effect on the U.S. economy and, for that matter, the economy of the entire world. As expected, the reaction of the stock market was negative, and those who were forced to sell stocks to raise needed capital suffered losses they could not recoup.

Another good example was the so-called "Crash of October 19, 1987" when the market, as measured by the Dow Jones Industrial Average, fell more than 500 points in one day, due in part to a rumor of unprecedented selling due to program trading. Longer term investors were hardly affected by this short-term disaster, except "on paper," but many who were in need of liquidity at that time never fully recovered.

Even long-term investors in the stock market should maintain cash reserves from time to time. Exactly how much really depends on whether a given market is over or under valued. Often, the market gets ahead of itself, and stock prices anticipate more economic and corporate earnings growth than is justified by reasonable analysis.

Over the years, I have applied an overly simplified approach to judging whether or not the market is temporarily over valued. My rule of thumb is to observe the prevailing interest rate on long-term U.S. Treasury Bonds and to relate it to stock prices.

Money has value; this is axiomatic. But to determine what money is worth at any given time is not so simple. Nonetheless, there is a relationship of long-term money rates to the stock market. If long-term U.S. Treasury Bonds are available in the market at, say, an 8 1/2 percent return, this suggests that such bonds are selling at 12 times their expected earnings (100 (par) divided by 8.5). At such a time, if the Dow Jones Industrial Average is selling at more than 12 times next year's expected earnings, then there is a "red flag." Stocks may be overvalued. Viewed another way, one can compute the proper price/earnings ratio of the D.J.I.A. using the following guidelines:

Return on long term U.S. Treasury Bonds	Proper Price/Earnings Ratios
10%	10.0 times
9%	11.1 times
8%	12.5 times
7%	14.3 times
6%	16.7 times
5%	20 times

In the early 1960s, the Dow Jones Industrial Average sold as high as 21 times earnings. But, back then, investors could justify 17 or 18 times earnings because interest rates were much lower than they are today. Then, interest rates were in the 4 1/4 percent range, so money was capitalized at 20 to 25 times earnings.

My rule of thumb worked spectacularly for me in 1987. I did not anticipate the October 19 crash, and I claim that anybody who says he did is either lucky or prone to hyperbole. Indeed, no one envisioned the extent to which the market would decline. However, according to this rule of thumb stocks were selling way above the then value of bonds during the summer of 1987. And the reason was quite obvious, even at that time. Everybody was buying stocks—the public, the mutual funds, the institutions, and the foreigners. There was enormous demand in the marketplace and, although even I failed to predict such a dramatic correction, it was obvious that we had an over-valued market.

My response to this reality in the summer of 1987 was *not* to flee the market. Instead, I either reduced my clients' and my own exposure to the market, or I let cash available for investment accumulate because I no longer believed that the stock market represented a bargain. When the crash came, I was as surprised as anybody at the magnitude of the decline, but I was not overly astonished at the action of the market. The day after the crash, we had not only adjusted through this criterion, but

stocks were then selling at a big discount again, and were sta-
tistically cheap.   Accordingly, I put some of that money to
work again.   This rule of thumb gave me a very objective perspective from which to view the market.   And hindsight dem-
onstrates that it proved to be accurate.   This rule does not
protect an investor from being entrenched in either a bear or
bull market.   But it assists in helping avoid the trap of becoming overly emotional one way or another.

Of course, the relationship of stock prices to interest rates
does not always remain constant.   In periods of anticipation of
lower interest rates, stock prices may have already discounted
the future by selling at higher than so-called "proper prices,"
and vice versa.

But current interest rates coupled with what those rates
might do over the short term can help investors establish perspective about stock values, and why earnings may be currently overestimated or underestimated.   Normally, the best
time to be fully invested in the stock market is when earnings
are currently depressed but are expected to rise at the very
time that interest rates are high and can be expected to fall.
The converse is also true.   At a time of very high earnings and
expectations of higher interest rates, it is appropriate to establish cash reserves.   Most of the time, price/earnings ratios of
market averages will conform to long-term rates, but a discrep-
ancy of more than 20 percent in price/earnings ratios may signal either an over bought or oversold market.

It is folly for long-term investors to be either 100 percent
invested or 100 percent liquid.   Circumstances can change rap-
idly, and virtually no investor is nimble enough to be in or out
of the market at precisely the proper time.   For that reason, I
rarely suggest a cash reserve of more than 25 percent, and less
than 10 percent for truly long term stock investors.

Speaking of cash reserves, it is necessary to define the term
precisely.   Most would interpret it as uninvested cash.   But beyond this, I prefer to define it as cash on hand *plus* additional

cash the investor anticipates will be generated for investment (perhaps, among other things, through income to be compounded) over the next 12 months.

Therefore, for example, a portfolio with 10 percent in cash, but which is expected to generate another 5 percent within a year, can be said to have a reserve of 15 percent.

One common mistake people make is to invest such cash reserves in illiquid investments in order to obtain a superior rate of return. Generally speaking, when I consider cash as a reserve, I refer to cash in liquid form. All reserves should earn a rate of return, but to invest these reserves in assets which are tied up for months or years, can severely restrict flexibility. I would rather keep reserves in money market funds redeemable on a day to day basis than hold, for example, non-redeemable (except with penalty) certificates of deposit for a period of months. Discrepancies in rate of return are offset by availability of cash when needed. Many investors are more conscious of rate of return than the reasons for liquidity, and they find that even though they may be correct in establishing reserves, they are unable to act when the time arrives to do so.

There are some other considerations investors should contemplate concerning cash reserves, the proper level of such reserves, and how they are utilized.

One important consideration is the amount of risk a given investor is willing to withstand or that "threshold of pain" to which an investor is willing to submit, at least on a short-term basis.

It is rare that the stock market will decline by more than 25 percent within a 12-month period. Such a drop is deemed disastrous, and in the past 50 years it has happened on only a few occasions. It follows, then, that a portfolio with a 20-percent cash reserve and an 80-percent investment will realize a 20 percent overall portfolio loss if the investment declines in value by 25 percent. It also follows that a lower or higher cash reserve provides different degrees of risk. If an investor believes he cannot psychologically withstand a substantial short-term decline in market value, he should keep reserves high, but also recognize that cash reserves will dilute the portfolio's potential for profits.

chapter 15

options

"I can't afford to sell."

I hear this statement by many investors who, despite market volatility, continue to hold on to stocks which they purchased at prices much lower than those prevailing today. Such investors are loath to sell because, by doing so, they would incur a tax bite on capital gains. Yet, they would like to sell in order to avail themselves of higher returns from other investments.

Is there a solution? Obviously, one alternative is to do nothing with the hope that share prices and dividends will increase. But there is still another alternative available to those who hold most quality securities: the sale of covered call options against those stocks. Contrary to many of my peers, I strongly endorse utilizing this strategy to increase cash flow and to mitigate declines in the value of my stock portfolio. Options provide a return substantially above dividends and afford a constant stream of cash flow for either reinvestment or spending purposes.

Although many investors consider options only for their more conventional function of hedging, it is prudent to focus on their cash flow value. Premiums from these options can be quite attractive, thus affording investors, in many cases, an annualized return on their stocks of 10 percent or more from option premiums plus dividends. Consistent with my philosophy of obtaining cash flow from every conceivable source, I rely heavily on options to add to my bottom line.

When people ask me what I think of options, I tell them that they provide a useful means of selling something that should end up worthless and getting paid for it. In fact, properly selling out-of-the-money covered options against long-term stock positions can be somewhat akin to taking candy from a baby.

What risks are involved? Contrary to the naysayers and skeptics who would have everyone avoid options altogether, there is virtually no risk of losing capital from the sale of certain options within a well defined strategy. However, there are two associated risks, in addition to the obvious risk of loss of additional opportunity. The first is the forced sale of a stock due to the exercise of the option. Another is the limitation of potential capital gain. But, with proper management and a predetermined plan of action, investors can minimize these risks.

Rather than being inordinately speculative, the sale or "writing" of covered options is generally viewed as a conservative strategy. Of course, this conservatism is offset by the seller's speculative counterpart, the buyer, who purchases the option because, for a small amount of money he can "control" a large amount of stock.

Why, then, do many investors shun options altogether? Why do they fear a tool which can increase cash flow and, at least to some extent, hedge unfavorable fluctuations in stock prices? There are several reasons, not the least of which is a belief that options per se are "speculative." There is also a lack of understanding of how stock options work.

More to the point, however, I have observed that most investors opt to remain passive with their stock holdings and are unwilling to spend either the time or effort to follow and manage their portfolios. Making money should be the main objective of all investors, and active management is vital to maximizing results.

BACKGROUND ON OPTIONS

Understanding options is the first hurdle in their proper employment as an investment tool. Although options can trace their existence back several centuries, it was not until 1973 that standardized, exchange listed, government regulated options became available. Since then, such instruments have displaced their over-the-counter equivalents, which used to comprise the bulk of the industry. Increasingly, options are also becoming a fixture in the emerging European and Asian stock exchanges, which are hungry for additional financial products.

Stock options listed in the U.S. are regulated by the SEC (Securities and Exchange Commission) and are traded on the major U.S exchanges, including the Chicago Board Options Exchange and the New York, American, Philadelphia, and Pacific Stock Exchanges. Each exchange provides a competitive, liquid, and orderly market for the purchase and sale of these instruments.

All option contracts traded on U.S. exchanges are issued, guaranteed, and cleared by a self-regulating organization called the OCC (Options Clearing Corporation). The OCC serves a vital function in guaranteeing that the terms of an option contract will be honored. Prior to the existence of options exchanges and the OCC, an option holder who wanted to exercise his instrument depended solely on the ethical and financial integrity of the issuer, or his brokerage firm. Many investors who tried to collect the option "premium" ultimately discovered that the issuer was unable to fulfill the obligation. The OCC ensures that such financial problems do not occur.

WHAT IS AN OPTION?

A stock option is a contract which gives the purchaser the right, but not the obligation, either to buy or sell shares of an underlying security at a fixed price, for a specified period of time. Likewise, the seller of an option is obligated either to sell or buy the shares to or from the buyer of the option at the specified price upon the option holder's request.

Because options have a limited life span, they are a "wasting asset." They can lose initial value and decline in price as time passes toward expiration. After the expiration date, the option ceases to exist.

Options are categorized as either "calls" or "puts," the calls conveying to their holders the right to buy an underlying security, and the puts offering holders the right to sell an underlying stock. Most stock option contracts are for 100 shares of the underlying stock.

> Example: An ABC Corporation April 50 Call entitles the buyer to purchase 100 shares of ABC Corporation stock at $50 per share at some time prior to the option's expiration date in April. Similarly, an April 50 Put entitles the buyer to sell 100 shares of ABC Corporation at $50 per share at some time before the option's expiration date. Consequently, if the price of the ABC April 50 Call is quoted at $5, the investor should expect to pay $500 ($5 x 100), plus commissions.

Several factors ascribe value to an option contract, thus influencing the "premium," or price at which it is traded. The most important factors are the price of the underlying stock, the strike price of the option, the time remaining until the expiration of the particular option, and the volatility of the underlying stock. The most critical determinant of any option's value is the price of its underlying stock.

If the price of the stock is above a call option's strike price, the call option is said to be "in-the-money." For example, if a call option's strike price is $50 and the underlying shares are trading at $60, the option has an "intrinsic value" of $10 because the holder of that option could exercise the option and buy the shares at $50. The buyer could then immediately sell shares on the stock market for $60, yielding a profit of $10 per share, or $1,000 per option contract.

STRIKE PRICE

The strike price of an option is the share price at which the shares of stock will be bought or sold if the owner exercises his option. Depending on the market price of the underlying security, strike prices are commonly listed in increments of 2 1/2, five, or ten points.   At any given time, an investor can buy or sell an option with one of four expiration dates. This standardization enables anyone to obtain option prices quickly and easily at any time during trading hours.   Major newspapers publish daily closing option prices, which buyers and sellers establish on regulated exchanges.

LEVERAGE

One of the most attractive features which options afford is leverage, which enables investors to take positions on large amounts of stock with minimal capital. The right to purchase or sell 100 shares of a particular stock at a specific price can be accomplished for a percentage of what an investor would pay or receive if trading the stock outright. This leverage allows the option investor to increase his potential benefit from small movements in a stock's price.

> xample: An investor is considering the purchase of 100 shares of XYZ trading at $50 per share, for a total of $5,000 plus commissions. Buying a $5 XYZ call option with a strike price of $50 would give him the right to buy 100 shares of the same stock any time during the life of the option for only $500 plus commissions.
>
> One month after the investor purchases the call option, the stock price rises to $55, resulting in a gain on the stock investment of $500 ($5 x 100 shares), or 10 percent . However, for the same $5 increase in the stock price, the call option premium might increase to $7, for a return of $200, or 40 percent.

Although the dollar amount gained on the stock investment is greater than the option investment, the percentage return is usually much greater with options than with stocks because of the effect of leverage.

COVERED CALL WRITING

As I have mentioned, one common use of options which I utilize and recommend is the sale of calls against an existing stock position. This strategy is a potent ally in my quest for increasing cash flow from every conceivable source. Remember, the key is to keep money flowing to you, and on an ongoing basis.

The seller of covered calls obligates himself to sell, at the specific strike price, his underlying shares of stock when the call buyer decides to exercise his option. For assuming this obligation, the investor is paid a premium at the time he sells the call.

The "writer," or seller, of covered calls should be fundamentally bullish or neutral toward the underlying stock, and have at least one of two objectives. The first is to gain some protection from a decline in the stock price. The second objective is to make additional money on his underlying stock by earning income from the option premium. Both objectives should be of great interest to those looking to increase cash flow.

WRITING OPTIONS TO PROTECT A DECLINE IN UNDERLYING STOCK PRICE

Example: An investor buys 100 shares of ABC company stock, which is selling at $52 per share. Then the investor sells an April 55 call option while holding his stock, thus establishing a covered call position. By selling the April 55 call option, the investor receives $400. If ABC company stock is below 55 at April expiration, the call option that was sold expires worthless and the investor earns $400 that he originally received for writing the call. Thus he receives $400, or four points, of downside protection. That is, he can afford to have the ABC stock drop by four points and still break even on the total transaction.

It is noteworthy that in the example above, if the stock of ABC corporation declines by more than four points, and the investor continues to hold his stock, he will still stand to lose on the overall position. Therefore, price risk appears in this strategy if the stock fell by an amount greater than the investor received from the original call option.

WRITING OPTIONS TO PROFIT ON AN INCREASE IN UNDERLYING STOCK PRICE

Example: Let's say that the stock of ABC increases moderately to 54 at the time of expiration of the April 55 call option. In this situation, the call will expire worthless and the investor will make $400 from the option in addition to the profit from his underlying stock. Moreover, the investor continues to hold the stock and stands to profit further from any additional price increase.

If, however, ABC increases in price to levels well above 55, the covered writer will have a number of alternatives from which to choose. First, he can do nothing, in which case the option will be exercised and his stock will be called away at the strike price of 55. Consequently, his profits will total the $400 he received from selling the call, plus the profit on the increase of his stock from the purchase price of 52 up to 55. In this case, he no longer holds the stock.

Second, if the investor chooses to retain his stock, he can buy back the call position in the open market, which could involve taking a loss on the option portion of the covered writing transaction. However, the investor would also stand to make a correspondingly larger profit from his underlying stock.

If the stock of ABC company rises to 65 by the expiration of the 55 April call option, the option will still be selling at an intrinsic value of 10 (the difference between the two strike prices), or $1,000 ($10 x 100). If the investor buys back his call at 10, he will lose $600 on the option portion of his option transaction ($1,000 paid, minus the $400 received). However, even if the investor chooses to buy back the option on the open market for $1,000, his profit on the underlying stock is an unrealized $1,300 ($65 - $52, or $13 x 100 shares), giving him a net profit on the strategy of $700 ($1,300 made on stock minus $600 paid for option).

Generally, covered call writing is a more conservative strategy than outright stock ownership because the investor's downside risk is partially offset by the premium he receives from selling the call. A covered call writer owns the underlying stock but is willing to surrender price increases in excess of the option strike price in return for the premium.

Investors should be prepared to deliver the required shares if the stock rises above the strike price at any time during the life of the option. Of course, an investor may always cancel his obligation at any time prior to receiving an assignment notice by buying back the call in the marketplace.

A covered call writer's potential profits and losses are determined by the strike price of the call he chooses to sell. In all cases, the writer's maximum net potential gain will be realized if the stock price is at or above the strike price of the option at expiration.

SOME GUIDELINES

I have three rules for optimizing this strategy.

First, I always sell six-month call options and avoid the shorter term instruments. One reason for this is that the premiums are larger for options with more time value—hence a higher rate of cash flow. Another reason is that multiple transactions cost money. Longer term options mean fewer trades and lower commission costs over time.

My second rule of thumb is that the *net* premium I receive, after commissions, *plus* the dividend, *plus* the appreciation (if the stock reaches the strike price), must yield an annualized rate of twice the going interest rate. In other words, if prevail-

ing interest rates are 10 percent, in exactly six months the total
return should be a rate of 10 percent (or 20 percent annually).
Likewise, if there is a period when annual interest rates are 6
percent, investors should want a 12 percent total return. In
short, they should plan to double the prevailing interest rate.
And people should be very happy, indeed, to make twice the
going interest rate on their money, year in and year out.

> Example: In choosing which General Electric option to sell,
> investors should undertake the above exercise, not necessar-
> ily looking for the biggest premium they can obtain. If GE
> is at 75, what they know is that if they sell a GE 80 call option
> due in six months at 2, they have automatically made 10
> percent if the stock gets to the strike price. They will not
> have to worry about the dividend.

> But if they sell a GE 70, they have to worry whether it is
> worth while to sell it. They will get more of a premium for
> the 70 call, but they may not meet their 20 percent an-
> nualized return.

I see all kinds of computer print-outs from very sophisticated research firms on how to pick the right option date and
the right strike price and the right stock. But my advice is
"forget it." The best strategy is usually the simplest. I know
what I want to accomplish with the sale of covered options,
and if I can accomplish this, I will be satisfied. Again, it is an
oversimplified rule of thumb. I may double the going rate on
money, if all works out. If it fails to materialize, and if General
Electric does not rise to the strike price I sold, this will work to
my advantage also. I have made more money than I would
have made by remaining passive and doing nothing.
My final rule kicks in if the stock goes through the strike
price. At this point, I buy back the option and keep the stock.
What I know, without performing analysis, is that the premium is infinite on an out-of-the-money option, but narrows

on the in-the-money option. So, I buy the option back if the stock goes through the strike price, and then I make up my mind whether or not I want to sell the stock.

Meanwhile, it is quite possible that I have lost money on the option. Indeed, I fervently hope so, which is something that is hard to convey to most people. I *hope* that by selling that option I lose money on it, because if I *do*, I will have made much more on the stock than I lost on the option. Since the option has been sold at a premium to what it is worth, the stock will increase in value much more than the option. It can shape up to be a classic no-lose or win-win situation.

Since the marketplace always presents uncertainties (and corresponding opportunities), conservative investors, particularly those who are "locked in" to a stock, should seriously consider the use of stock options. There is only one reason to own a stock: to make money. Why not take advantage of all that is available in the marketplace? Decisions about what to buy, what to sell, or what to hold are not always self-evident, but wisely managing what one holds can produce additional profitable results.

Options have become increasingly important investment tools for supplementing cash flow and enhancing portfolio returns. Rather than avoiding options because they are "speculative," it is better to exploit their more sophisticated use with conservative strategies. It is also a good idea to keep in mind that the *buyer* of an option, not the seller, is the real speculator in the covered call option strategy. Eventually, at expiration, most options become worthless. For this reason, investors should avoid buying "put" options as a hedge against declines in stock prices because paying premiums *reduces* cash flow, and runs counter to a comprehensive strategy to *increase* overall cash flow.

The value of a covered call program has not escaped the purview of modern portfolio managers. If the primary objective of such a program is to increase income, it follows that a portfolio which includes covered call writing should consistently outperform outright stock ownership. Furthermore, evidence suggests that the consistent and conservative use of writing covered call options against a stock position can have a measurable impact in lowering long-term *variability* of portfolio returns. In effect, this strategy can become a perpetual windfall for those investors who avail themselves of this important tool.

chapter **16**

mutual funds

There is an old saying in Wall Street that mutual funds are sold, not bought. Indeed, the mutual fund industry and the brokerage community have done a magnificent job of selling these products to the public, and the public has come to perceive mutual funds as *the* right way to invest. But, in fact, a deeper analysis reveals that the public has been misled, having been sold a bill of goods.

Contrary to public opinion, mutual funds are not the best vehicle through which to invest money. In fact, I contend that several problems with the funds themselves make them poorer investments than individual stocks. Admittedly, this viewpoint may rub industry insiders and mutual fund investors the wrong way. But although people would like to think they have chosen correctly by investing in these products, experience (and performance) might teach them that they are wrong or, at least, not as right as they should be.

Statistics show that the mutual fund industry exploded in popularity during the 1980s, most certainly to the detriment of many investors. Numbers also suggest that shareholders have not made expected windfall profits through mutual funds, except as the market itself has performed well. The Lipper Organization regularly publishes average mutual fund performance reported by types of funds. Invariably, the average fund returns somewhat less than the market itself.

Back in 1987, when everyone was jumping on the mutual fund bandwagon, investors chose probably the worst time to climb on board. Certainly during October of that year the funds were hit harder than most other investments. It is also fair to say that during the crash of 1987 mutual funds compounded the problem of volatility, and there is no reason to believe that a like event today would not yield similar results. During that crash, it was not only institutions that sold heavily, it was also the program trading mutual funds. And, as the market declined, the programmers sold until the stocks literally flooded the marketplace, thus emerging as a major culprit of the crash. But, as disastrous as it was, the crash did little damage to the individual investor who was not forced to sell. When the mutual funds were forced to sell, however, it was very hard for them to bounce back.

Generally speaking, mutual funds have less control over their destinies than most people realize because they affect the overall market when they sell. The individual investor can sell 100 or 500 shares with very little problem. But the mutual fund has a problem trying to sell 100,000 shares in a crash market. In fact, large sell orders are virtually impossible to execute efficiently; when they are, they adversely affect the prices at which the mutual fund can sell.

PROBLEMS WITH MUTUAL FUNDS

Reading a prospectus for a mutual fund can be an exercise in futility. One gets the feeling that the legal profession has crafted these convoluted documents to perpetuate the species known as the securities attorney. Within these mutual fund prospectuses are several explicit and implicit disclosures which most investors rarely observe. Of course, the mutual fund itself is buying and selling securities and is incurring transaction costs, which are relatively nominal because these funds are institutional investors and obtain breaks on commissions for the purchase and sale of individual securities.

Next, most mutual funds assess fees for entering into and redeeming shares. And even no-load funds have on-going operational expenses. The result is a dilution of both capital and income for the investor. Then, add the management cost, which comes out of either the income or the capital of the fund. Depending on the type of fund, fees can range from between 15 to 20 percent of income. The no-load fund is certainly no improvement, assessing higher annual expenses than its front load counterpart.

Breaking it down further, a $100 million mutual fund may realize earnings at a rate of 3 percent per year. This is strictly dividend income of $3 million. The annual cost of the management of that fund, which comes out of the fundholders' income, is about 15 to 20 percent of that $3 million. It is self-evident that over a 20-year period, expenses can translate to enormous capital, which has not been working for the investor. With compounding, it is a fairly substantial amount and varies depending on the kind of fund. Growth funds normally access a higher percentage of income than income funds. On average, costs can be roughly three quarters of one percent per year of the value of the fund.

Mutual fund fees are severe when compared to the simple purchase of General Electric stock, for example, at a relatively nominal commission rate with no residual charge.

WHICH MUTUAL FUND?

Another problem is the difficulty in picking the *right* mutual fund, particularly since times change, and a given mutual fund manager may do well during one period of time but not fare well in another. I have had investors walk into my office and demand, "Find me the right mutual fund." My comeback to that kind of statement is that I am not proficient enough to figure out the right mutual fund to buy for the next five or ten years. In fact, it is virtually impossible to do so. It is less of a problem locating individual stocks that are good investments for the next five or ten years, than locating mutual funds. The reasons are two-fold. First, no one has an idea of how these funds will do in the future. Second, few investors ever thoroughly consider the net effect of a mutual fund on their long-term objectives and tax obligations.

If an investor buys the shares of a mutual fund which has performed very well over the past, and presumably will do well in the future, the IRS might still hit him with unexpected tax liability. Take the mutual fund that bought IBM at $10 a share and sold at $100. Although the investor did not buy in at $10 dollars a share, the fund did. The result is that the profit is then passed on to each investor in the form of a capital gain on which taxes are assessed. Thus, the investor loses control of his own destiny when he buys a mutual fund. Most investors like to control their own destinies—i.e., when they take profit, when they absorb a loss, and how they invest their money over time. Mutual funds obviate these decisions, with the result that investors tend to lose flexibility. By the time they realize the error of their ways, it is usually too late. The fund has already taken the action that reverberates through to their bottom line.

If people are savvy enough to be able to pick the *right* mutual fund from the various funds that are available—and actually there are more mutual funds available than there are stocks listed on the New York Stock Exchange—they have to be consummate geniuses. In order to pinpoint the particular mutual fund that will outperform other funds, and the stock market generally, an investor has to know something about the fund's management team and about the style of investing that will be beneficial to performance *for that investor.* Furthermore, he has to know about the stocks in which the fund will be investing. Logically, it follows that if an investor knows all of this, he certainly knows the right individual stocks to buy on his own.

Having confronted the problem of picking the right fund, the potential buyer then faces the possibility that a manager may alter his trading style with the evolving market environment. Past performance is very often a moot issue as a given style may not do as well (or as poorly) in the future as it has done in the past, and as times and economic conditions change. The critical problem for the buyer of a mutual fund is that he has no way of knowing how his manager may trade in the future and what effect such a trading style might have on his individual investment objectives.

OTHER PROBLEMS

It is my general observation that mutual funds are over-diversified. With veritable billions to invest, these funds have no choice but to over-diversify. And, it is a well-established principle that over-diversification is a sure path to mediocre performance.

Mutual funds are also forced to do the wrong things at the wrong time, even though the manager recognizes it to be wrong. In a very strong stock market, cash comes into the mutual funds that are doing well and the managers of the funds are forced to buy stocks at unreasonably high levels. I recall that during the summer of 1987, capital flooded into the mutual funds just when investors should have been looking to pull out. Conversely, in bad markets, investors are prone to cash in their chips and head for the exits, and the money manager is forced to sell stocks to pay redemptions. Thus, there is an inherent timing problem for the mutual fund manager, which precludes him from investing as he ought.

As a money manager, I sympathize with the enormous problems confronting fund managers. It is a formidable problem when the psyche of the investor is not as contrarian as it needs to be, especially in difficult trading environments. At the point at which mutual fund managers should be purchasing additional stocks, because they know the prices are right, they find that the investors are redeeming shares of the fund, impeding efforts to buy more low-priced shares. Consequently, instead of buying, fund managers are forced to sell during the most inopportune moments.

Another negative factor with mutual funds is that investors cannot sell options against these funds, and if part of one's strategy is to utilize the options market in order to enhance cash flow or to hedge the price of a security, mutual funds will eliminate a vital part of this strategy. Funds inhibit the full range of possibilities that an investor might have. It is possible that a particular mutual fund manager might be selling covered options within the fund. But the drawback is that this strategy is not necessarily for the benefit of the *given investor*, as such.

Why is it, then, that the brokers sell these products? Well, for starters, the commissions are usually attractive. Second, if the mutual fund performs poorly, the broker has a scapegoat.

He can say, "Well, it wasn't *my* fault, it was the fault of the mutual fund manager. Let's sell that one and buy another."

ADVANTAGES OF MUTUAL FUNDS

Having cast a palpable cloud of gloom on this industry, it is important to note that mutual funds *do* offer some advantages and have their role for specific purposes. For example, if an investor feels that he or she ought to have an investment in foreign stocks but is unable to follow individual foreign securities, then an international mutual fund might make sense for a portion of his money. Likewise, if an investor is looking to place a portion of his money in so-called "emerging growth stocks," mutual funds offer a way to obtain a diversified list of these stocks without spending inordinate time and effort analyzing small companies. Such analysis is demanding work, even for professionals.

In addition to the international and emerging growth funds, there are other "special situation" funds which help achieve specific investment objectives. For example, some mutual fund families offer special industry funds for those who want to have a certain percentage of their money in, say, energy stocks, but cannot find the right stocks. If such an investor does not have enough money to be diversified, then an energy mutual fund might make sense. But, again, it is usually wiser to buy the Atlantic Richfields and the Exxons of this world than a widely diversified energy fund, particularly when investing for the long run.

There is still another important reason to own mutual funds. For the very small investor who wants to dollar average into the market with a small amount of money, funds offer a very convenient way of periodically investing less capital into the market on a dollar-averaging basis.

In the final analysis, however, the argument for and against buying into mutual funds betrays a deeper confusion among investors, many of whom categorically refuse to trust themselves, believing instead that the big fund managers are omniscient. In fact, fund results should lead one to the opposite conclusion. Fund managers are human beings and are subject to the same mistakes as others in the investment of money. It is my observation that people, generally, do not trust their own instincts or their ability to choose individual stocks themselves; if they did, they would be much better off. It is always easier to hand off or to defer to someone who is perceived to have more experience. But, like anything else, the more time one devotes to studying the market, the better he will perform—always. This is as true in the investment world as it is in any business. One should not assume that the manager of a mutual fund is a variation of a genius.

In the case of a Peter Lynch, however, there is a real benefit in choosing a money manager who really sinks his teeth into the analysis of companies, their products and their balance sheets. Indeed, the Fidelity Magellan Fund has been a classic exception to my bias against mutual funds. The good performance of this fund, which was one of the best of the 1980s, was due to Peter Lynch. What happened, however, was that in the first part of 1990, Peter decided to retire from the management of that fund, and the holder of that fund no longer had that "particular genius" managing his money. Also, many unsuspecting shareholders who redeemed shares of the Magellan Fund discovered that the IRS had also noticed the fund's spectacular performance and taxed them accordingly. And herein lies a pitfall: although this fund, or any other similar product, has an outstanding manager, the fund itself does not provide the individual the necessary flexibility for *his own particular financial situation* as it evolves, and yet there is a difficulty in adjusting investment strategy if locked into a fund.

It is important to recognize that when anyone purchases individual stocks, he is really purchasing the ability of a money manager. Chief executives of corporations are essentially no more and no less than money managers. They manage the money of that particular company, and the purchaser of stock is buying the expertise of the chairman of the board of that company. When I buy General Electric, for example, I buy into the management expertise of that company. Why put faith in an unknown manager of a mutual fund? So often people look at the past performance of a mutual fund in those glossy sales packages and say, "that's the right fund to own." But past performance is just that—*past* performance. It is not necessarily indicative of future returns.

When invested in the stock of a corporation, one does not have to worry about this quite so much. It is a truism that good management breeds good management, and a corporation which has been managed well in the past can be expected to do well in the future. General Electric is a good example. This firm has always had good management, even though the names have changed.

For special situation investing, perhaps a mutual fund is suitable, but it is still not the best way to invest money. It is far better to buy the shares of one good quality stock and reinvest dividends for a total return.

Not long ago, a young man came into my office and said "I want your advice." He said, "I'm 40 years old, and I have only $10,000 to invest. However, I'm making good money and I *could* put away about $500 a month. My goal is to accumulate money toward my retirement at the age of 60 or 65, or whatever it may be. What would you advise?"

My first piece of advice was, given that kind of time horizon, I would want to be in equities rather than in fixed-income investments. Second, I would want to be in growth stocks rather than in income-producing stocks. And third, I would rather own two or three fairly obvious stocks. With $10,000 anyone can open up a brokerage account and buy himself a few shares of stocks like General Electric or some of the very obvious blue chips. He can deposit $500 into the account each month, along with the dividends and, as money accumulates, buy additional shares of those stocks on a dollar averaging basis.

It is predictable that over the next 20 years, those stocks will increase and decrease in value, depending on market conditions. But it is also true that the account will generate cash flow not only from dividends, but also from the deposits made in the account. And the reinvestment on a compounded, dollar averaging basis can offset timing problems.

The commissions are relatively low, even paying 2 or 3 percent on the relatively small purchases. This is less than one would pay on the purchase of most mutual funds. Yet, the stocks afford access to one of the best management teams in the world, companies with good track records behind them. This is not to say that those companies will not experience problems in the future. Indeed, they might. But so, too, might a mutual fund. Given a long-term time horizon, however, this strategy will likely outperform the market. In short, why should investors not own individual stocks of obvious quality, avoid expenses on a continual basis, and keep control over the way their money is invested? Indeed, I do not know a good answer to that question.

insights from
a life on
wall street

chapter

a few
misconceptions

People believe whatever they hear or read, which can sometimes lead them to irrational conclusions. Below are some of
the more intriguing theories which I have encountered.

THE NATIONAL DEFICIT

Consider the cry of the day: "Uncle Sam is broke." By this
most mean that the federal government is spending more than
it takes in, is running an enormous deficit, has a high debt, and
that therefore, the future of America has been mortgaged, leaving no room for economic growth.

There is no question that Washington has been spending
heavily, that the "pork barrel" system of government is one
good reason for this, that the federal deficit remains at record

levels, and that the national debt balloons higher and higher each day. But has it reached catastrophic levels? Not really.

For starters, consider that Uncle Sam's accounting system is quite different from yours and mine. Uncle Sam operates on a "cash flow" basis, not a profit/loss basis. When he spends money to buy an office building or an aircraft carrier, it is considered a current expense, not a capital outlay.

When Uncle Sam spends on defense, many assume it is a net expense. Not so. Remember that he recoups some of this through taxation of profits on defense contracts, taxation of the income of people employed in the defense sector, taxation of the profits of merchants who sell to those employees,and so on. And the same is true of spending in other areas.

Unfortunately, Uncle Sam does not produce a true balance sheet showing assets held (which have value) against liabilities owed. If he did, the U.S. Government would show a strong "book value."

The $2 trillion plus debt of the federal government is a figure which boggles the minds of most people. But consider the fact that the debt level is not as much as the annual gross income, that the debt service cost is only about 15 percent of revenue (and that even some of this flows back to Uncle Sam in the form of taxes on interest received by the lenders), and that most of the debt the U.S. creates is offset by assets acquired. For sure, federal deficits are one cause of inflation, but debt and excessive spending in the private sector is much more culpable.

Compare Uncle Sam's balance sheet and income statement with that of the average family. Suppose, for example, that a family has annual net income of $50,000, owns a home worth $200,000, and, holds other assets amounting to $100,000. Suppose, further, that the family has a mortgage on its home of $100,000 (interest at 9 percent) and other debt of $10,000 (interest at 15 percent). By anyone's standards (certainly the standards of most lending institutions), this is a well-financed family with good income. And yet, its annual interest costs are over 20 percent of its income, and its debt is high relative to its assets. Uncle Sam is much stronger than that, and furthermore, although Uncle Sam's income and expenses may fluctuate from time to time, he will not lose his job nor his assets because of temporary economic conditions.

I abhor the increases in the national deficit and national debt, not because they are extreme but because the government is failing to address the necessity of "keeping some powder dry" to offset unforeseen contingencies such as war, disasters of all kinds and deep, long-lasting recessions. In fact, the irony in all of this is that the deficits have gone way up during times of greatest prosperity. But the alternatives of reducing government services and benefits and/or greatly increasing taxes are neither popular nor acceptable.

In the meantime, those who do not invest their money in income and capital growth assets because of their fears of Uncle Sam's fiscal policies are destined for disillusionment.

ONE BIG CASINO

It is often said that the stock market is essentially "one great big casino," and that to make money in the market one has to be lucky. Well, there is nothing wrong with being lucky. I have known many investors who bought a stock for one reason but made money on it (or lost, for that matter) for another reason altogether.

But the mainstream of the movement of the stock market is not luck. Instead, it is a reflection and a prediction of economic trends and, as we have explained, is a reaction to earnings and dividends as they occur or can be perceived to occur. Remember, it is not through luck that market prices multiplied by 15 times over the last 40 years.

THE VOLATILE MARKET

Most people would say that the stock market is more volatile today than it has ever been. This premise is patently false. In fact, stock price volatility was much higher *relative to market performance* during the decades preceding the 1980s than in the 1980s themselves (See Figure 4).

It is possible, although experience belies this, that while long-term volatility is lower now, short-term volatility is higher. We have witnessed many days when the Dow Jones Industrial Average has gone up or down 100 points and, to most, this seems volatile. But considering the level of stock prices, it is not as volatile as many believe.

Perhaps the recent advent of program trading, whereby institutions automatically buy or sell millions of shares simul-

Figure 4   Dow Jones Industrials vs. Volatility

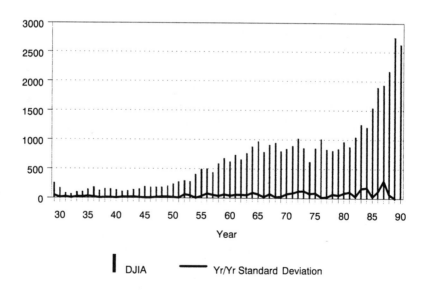

taneously, has increased short-term volatility. But this is almost self-correcting and, in fact, one can argue that program trading serves to counter irrational price movements, thereby acting as a stabilizer rather than a producer of price swings. Although no one can draw a definitive conclusion on this subject, people try to point out that program trading is "unfair to the average investor." I remain skeptical as to exactly why or how that may be true except, perhaps, to the extent that program trading may inhibit short-term trading ability. But, as I have said, the word "programs" should not be a part of the average investor's vocabulary anyway.

BUYOUTS

During the 1980s, a whole generation of investors was taught that the way to make money in the stock market was to ferret out companies which were "buyout" candidates, buy their stocks, and then sell them way above their value to the so-called "sharks" of Wall Street, or those engaged in leveraged buyouts.

It was certainly a way to make money during the 1980s if investors picked the right stocks at the right times. But the air was full of rumors and "hot tips" about which companies would be bought and, unfortunately, for every one that worked out there were a dozen which failed. In the meantime, investors were induced to buy shares of relatively low-grade companies at what turned out to be very high prices.

If hindsight teaches us anything, it is that buying stocks on rumors of mergers and speculation of short-term price movements is fraught with peril. My advice is to buy the fairly and/or undervalued stocks based on fundamental research, and then let the buyouts happen, rather than try to anticipate them. Contrary to popular opinion, the buyout specialists are not dumb, they *do* look for value, and they *do* walk away from over valued situations.

SPEND ONLY INCOME—NEVER CAPITAL

Entire generations have grown up believing that they should never spend capital, only income. But times have changed, and people should think differently. We should disregard the difference between capital and income, and insist that the totality of money is the important reality. Income can and should be converted into capital, and such capital is not sacrosanct from being spent from time to time.

The British came to this conclusion long ago. For generations, the British passed on annuities rather than set income interests, as inheritances. In historic novels, like David Copperfield, one can read lines such as, "He had so many quid and so much income per year as his inheritance." This was a total return concept, well before the term "total return" was in vogue.

Indeed, the David Copperfields of the world never received "so many pounds in trust." Instead, they always had so much income per year—*money to spend per year*. Likewise, we should think in terms of converting income into more income-producing capital. And to the extent that we use money, we should also stop worrying about whether that money is in the form of interest, dividends, or capital. It is one and the same.

Unfortunately, this pattern of thinking, whereby investors segregate capital, interest, and dividends still exists today, particularly in the trust business. Trust documents will include such language as, "Mr. Smith leaves what he has in trust—the income—to Mrs. Smith, so long as she shall live." If the income is insufficient, that's too bad, because the capital is off limits to Mrs. Smith.

Such thinking severely constrains an effective investment program, because the important thing should be to provide Mrs. Smith her daily bread. Beyond this, the trusts are normally invested to produce a high level of income instead of capital growth, and this is to the detriment of the subsequent heirs. If there were more flexibility in the management of that money, that capital could be invested on a *total* return basis, with a portion of that total return going to Mrs. Smith for bread and butter, but with the remainder reinvested for the benefit of the heirs, the world would be better off.

Separating capital from income results in a conflict of interest in an investment strategy. It is encouraging to note that some lawyers and trust companies are becoming more flexible in their approach to money management. This bodes well for the future.

JUNK BONDS

Although my advice to most investors is to steer clear of so-called junk bonds or mutual funds which invest in them, not all junk bonds are created equal.

In fact, analytically minded investors, and those who have both the expertise and the time to devote to analysis, can find good values in low-quality bonds, those of highly leveraged companies, and those of relatively small companies which are not rated. And, from time to time, bondholders of bankrupt companies can experience windfalls as a result of reorganization plans.

Many investors buy junk bonds just because their interest rates are high or their prices low. This is a good way to lose money, both income and capital. But fortunes have been made by those who can analyze statements, observe legal quirks in a bond indenture, or anticipate legal decisions made by bankruptcy judges. This is not my area of expertise, but I commend those for whom it is.

INSIDER MANIPULATION

For many reasons, investors sometimes say that the stock market is rigged, that the insiders control it, that only the "big boys" can make money on Wall Street, and that, therefore, the average investor loses out.

It is certainly true that in recent years there has been rash of illegal activities in the marketplace, ranging from insider trading and illegal "parking of securities," to public misinformation and alleged manipulation of U.S. Treasury Bond prices. Names like Boesky, Milkin, and others have hit the headlines with unprecedented regularity.

There is little question that large buyers and sellers of securities can and do influence prices; there is also little doubt that there have been many abuses in the marketplace, both legal and illegal. But the Securities and Exchange Commission (SEC) and the investment banking industry have done a magnificent job of regulating the investment markets and pursuing and punishing illegal activities.

The rigging of markets today takes place with less frequency and impact than used to be the case during the heydays of the so-called "Robber Barons." Laws are stronger and regulations are stricter. As a matter of fact, when people point to market abuses, they often overlook the mainstream of the securities markets. The mainstream is a market where literally millions of transactions—both large and small—take place every day, and the great majority of them as a result of verbal contracts. By and large, the securities industry maintains a high level of integrity, with the occasional exceptions hitting the headlines and clouding the perception.

Speaking of insider activity, some believe that observation of "insider trading activity" can give clues as to whether or not to buy or sell a given stock or stocks. The SEC mandates that corporate executives report purchases and sales of the stocks of their companies. The names of these executives and their trading activities are published in leading business journals.

In fact, insider trading is rarely a good gauge of whether to buy or sell. Insiders trade for many reasons. They may be exercising options, they may be selling to raise liquid funds for whatever reason. Or, of course, they may be buying or selling because they surmise their stocks are either undervalued or overvalued. But insiders are not necessarily experts on what their stocks may do in the market. Of course, investors should hope and expect that directors and officers of a company own stock in that company, but just the fact that a few executives buy or sell is not a sufficient reason for investment decision-making on the part of an individual investor.

LOOK FOR SHORT-TERM PLAYS

The great bulk of investors read about why the market went up or down and they make an assumption that their investment decisions should be based on short-term considerations. These may include what the Federal Reserve may do to adjust the money supply, what the Consumer Price Index (CPI) will reveal about inflation, or what the government may report about leading economic indicators. But the longer term decision of whether to buy or sell a stock should include more than simply a reaction to what is happening shorter term.

One day, the *Wall Street Journal* may report, "Oil prices are expected to rise because of tensions in the Middle East." The next day it might read, "Oil prices are expected to drop because of peace." The real winners in these announcements are the brokerage firms who squeeze the short-term trader with multiple commissions.

What people should ask themselves after reading those headlines is, "Do I want to be in the oil business for the long term?" The answer to that question, rather than what oil prices did yesterday or are going to do tomorrow, should prompt them to buy or sell that stock. The long-term question should be "Is oil *really* a good industry in which to be invested long term?" This applies to any industry or any company. As the current news of the day either evaporates or melds into the news of tomorrow, keeping an eye on the ball for the longer term becomes much more important.

BE A TRADER, NOT AN INVESTOR

Very few short-term traders consistently make much money. The only exception to the rule may be the brokerage firms which, in addition to trading profits or losses, also include mark-ups, mark-downs, and commissions as part of their profits. As a rule, individuals rarely make consistent money trading the markets. If they do, they may be lucky, as opposed to smart.

Commission costs alone can debilitate a good trader. If a trader buys a stock, holds it for a week and sells it, he has lost 4 percent via commissions. Then he has to decide what to do with the capital once he sells the stock, whereupon he pays another commission. In the end, if only one trade is wrong, the entire series of trades can realize net losses.

In the futures and options markets, where increased leverage can magnify gains and losses in a short time, traders know that 50 winning trades followed by one loser can wipe them out. These traders express this truth in a familiar, but crass colloquialism: "In this business," they say, "you masticate like a bird and defecate like an elephant." One bad trade can bury you.

Investors who try to be traders find they are unable to make money trading in the marketplace. Of course, some individuals who are exceptionally talented and disciplined do succeed. But they are the exception rather than the norm. The average investor cannot, and does not, spend as much time in the marketplace as he must to become a proficient trader.

One example of how the trader mentality has come to pervade the marketplace is the use of the "limit order." Investors, in their buying and selling habits, place limit orders on the prices for which they are willing to buy or sell. In doing so, they make a critical mistake. Sometimes it works and other times it does not.

With a limit order, one can buy a stock for less than it is now selling or sell a stock for more than it is now selling. But, consistent with a long-term strategy, it is always best to buy a stock regardless of its current price. Likewise, it is best to sell a stock without worrying about the price. An investor should want to be in the stock or out of it. Whether it is selling for 53, 53 1/2, or 54 makes little difference. The buyer wants the stock because he thinks it is going to go to 100; the seller wants out of it because he believes it is going to fall to 25. Yet, many people are so enamored of trying to fine-tune the prices at which they are willing to buy or sell, that they miss the bigger picture. The trading mentality that strives to squeeze the last quarter or the last half, or even the last point in the marketplace is, at best, myopic.

chapter **18**

brokers

A good money manager is often the beneficiary of sound advice, intelligent insights, and years of wisdom gleaned from experienced colleagues. Indeed, I am no exception. Throughout the years, I have been surrounded by some of the finest men and women in the business and have benefited greatly by their knowledge of markets and investments. I can only hope these friends have also gained in some way through this cross pollination of ideas.

In moments of nostalgia, however, I am sometimes prone to reminisce on the faded image of the hard core, cigar chomping stock brokers of yesteryear who donned green eye shades, armed themselves with sharp pencils, and prided themselves on bearing the latest stock tips. Alas, this image has been replaced with that of a vanilla flavored "jack of all trades and master of none," who dispenses the latest "kitschy" information on everything from tax-free mutual funds to limited partnerships in shrimp farms.

Indeed, some securities brokers have come to resemble door-to-door salesmen, trying to sell everyone on the block a new vacuum cleaner. When they arrive at your door and you tell them that you already have a reliable vacuum, they reach into their back pocket, pull out a monkey wrench and ask, "How about one of these?" Armed with a staggering array of financial products, like so many flavors of the week, brokers have become less experts in their fields than purveyors of the trendy "deal."

Nostalgia and sarcasm aside, it is my observation that the public has forgotten the true role of a stockbroker, which is the same as *any* broker. A broker is someone who represents someone else in the buying and selling of assets and who charges a commission for a transaction. Anything else is in addition to the brokerage function. Today, of course, in the full service brokerage industry we have added to that the function of dispensing advice. But it is not the advice for which the broker charges a commission; *it is the transaction.* This distinction is relevant because the person who charges a commission on a transaction is often inducing the transaction with advice. The incentive for a broker is to have a transaction, and the prudence or impropriety of that transaction is not necessarily uppermost in his mind.

In recent years, we have witnessed the emergence of financial planners who are paid on a fee basis. This method of compensation is preferable, but certainly not foolproof. The client pays for a service, the broker defines the value of that service, and the advisor may or may not have a vested interest in the transaction itself. The problem is that many investment advisors who charge a fee for financial planning also benefit from the transaction. Although this is a blatant conflict of interest, the fact remains that such planners are not immune from the tendency to lead investors toward a prejudice for the higher transaction fee.

My observation is that the great bulk of retail brokers—those who deal with individuals on a public basis—are not in-depth securities analysts. In fact, few of them even pretend to be. They are people trained to sell the ideas of their firm, which may range from research to suggestions for portfolio strategies.

The insidious part about client-broker relationships, is that there exists an overwhelming incentive to a broker to sell the investment which attaches the highest commission. As is true in any business where a product is sold, the thing on which one makes the most money is the thing he would most like people to buy. This is not necessarily dishonest, but it involves a covert incentive. These brokers should not be individually faulted for this predisposition; instead, perhaps the entire system should be faulted and corrected.

HOW TO CHOOSE A BROKER

A common problem with brokers or financial planners is that they tend to persuade their clients to invest in products with which they are most familiar. When talking to a financial planner who has most of his expertise in insurance, odds are overwhelming that at least part of his investment recommendations will involve the purchase of insurance of one kind or another. Likewise, when conferring with a planner associated with a trust company, it is likely that somewhere down the line he is going to recommend the use of trust services. In similar fashion, a commercial banker will probably favor some sort of deposit with the bank.

Those who employ consultants should take care to choose someone who has no ax to grind as far as the resultant transaction is concerned. Admittedly, this eliminates plenty of good advisors, but it also takes the prejudice out of the advice. This does not, however, eliminate the problem of the prejudice of the advisor toward the areas of his expertise. But people should look for advisors who admit their shortcomings, defer to others for information outside the area of their expertise, and focus on their strengths. I, for example, am prone to talk to investors about the stock and bond markets, but not about real estate investments nor the use of insurance, because these fall outside my purview. If my potential client wants a good real estate limited partnership, I recommend a broker who is well versed in such products. Nobody is an expert in everything. Anybody who says he is is probably lying or has an inflated ego.

In picking a broker, one thing I demand is a good "chemistry" between the two of us. I want a broker who knows my needs, my goals, and my desires. And I certainly don't want him to arrive at his conclusions based on a computer form that I may have filled out about my financial profile. Such forms are pedantic and shallow.

The broker should know what kind of service I want, what kind of service I need, what level of risk I can afford, and what kind of reward I am trying to achieve. Most important, he should know my psychological makeup. Understanding a client's psyche is important to being a good consultant, and unfortunately, not enough brokers care about this aspect of business; they care instead about whether they get a trade with the client. I want somebody who understands me and, to the extent I need help, can devote the time and energy to helping me on a transaction and in an advisory capacity. Of course, I also want someone with high integrity. *Whenever* I deal, I want to deal with people of high integrity, but this is a subjective sort of requirement. In any case, I also want an advisor with experience. Ten years of experience is almost insufficient. Having witnessed all kinds of markets, both good and bad, a seasoned advisor is much better able to recognize both risks and rewards of whatever advice he offers.

HOW TO CHOOSE A BROKERAGE FIRM

Investors should insist on certain imperatives in a brokerage firm. Among them is demonstrated financial stability. Most of them will *claim* that they have financial wherewithal, but this may not necessarily be the case. Almost all brokerage companies have SIPC insurance (Securities Investor Protection Corp.) which assures investors they will not lose money or the assets they hold at the firm. This is important, but not foolproof. If a brokerage firm goes out of business, investors may realize big delays in retrieving their assets. Some firms have filed for bankruptcy and clients have obtained their assets only after much travail. Red tape can tie up capital for months. It is a matter of knowing with whom one is dealing.

FULL SERVICE VS. DISCOUNT

One of the most important criteria in choosing a broker is the recognition of what an investor expects from him. Is it advice or is it execution of transactions? If the latter, it will probably cost less through a discount broker. Discount firms are not necessarily a preference, but they are certainly worth exploring if investors are making their own decisions. If they know what they want to buy or sell, and if they are making their decisions and can do without the advice of a broker, then they can save money with the discount broker.

Large institutions can usually save money with full service brokers, too, through negotiating rates based on volume. I, for example, obtain good commission discounts from full service brokers on behalf of my customers because I manage and trade large sums of money. But the relatively small investor has less leverage in negotiating rates than does the large institution.

There is also something to be said for the availability of a ready inventory of stocks and bonds by large full service firms, and their ability to offer the investor a better price for these securities. For the average investor who is buying or selling 100 or 200 shares of listed stock, this means very little. But if one is concentrating on over-the-counter stocks and a given broker makes a market in them, the investor may be able to get better prices with the larger brokerage firm. This is certainly true in the fixed-income area. Brokers who take positions in fixed-income instruments can provide better bids and offers because they can eliminate an extra charge for what they have to pay others to complete transactions.

Whether one chooses to use a regional broker or a large national "wire service" firm is a moot issue. There are good regional firms and good wire house firms and it is difficult to generalize on the benefits and liabilities of each. Again, it really depends upon the service one requires. If the main interest is in securities of a regional nature, the regional firm specializing in these securities may be the best, although some national firms follow regional companies as well.

RED FLAGS

One red flag that would send me somewhere else would be a broker who told me how good he was, or tried to hard-sell me into buying something without knowing anything about my circumstances. Despite the fact I am in the business, I receive numerous "cold calls" from brokers, and I have sympathy for people who make a hundred calls hoping to get three or four orders. But I watch out for anyone who calls me and says, "This is Joe Smith and I just want you to know that next week my firm is going to underwrite a bond issue of XYZ county in Minnesota, and I was wondering if you'd like to buy some bonds because they're probably going to yield 6 percent."

Immediately, I recognize that this is a securities huckster, not someone who necessarily has my best interests at heart.

Instead of thinking about *my* investment goals, he is thinking about selling *his* securities.

Another red flag is a broker who donates too many recommendations too often because he is obviously not motivated by a desire to have me invested the way I ought to be. This is known in the trade as "churning" a portfolio, and it is an expensive habit.

For *investors* in stocks, transaction costs in the securities industry are lower than they are in almost every other industry. Certainly in real estate, the transaction costs are *much* higher than they are in the securities industry. If you sell a house for $100,000, chances are that your real estate commission is $6000 or $7000. In the stock market, if you buy or sell a stock for $100,000 the commission probably is going to run $1,500—obviously a large disparity.

For *traders* of stocks, however, transactions can eliminate any chance for sustained profits over the long term. Not every broker who encourages multiple transactions is purposely churning a portfolio, but it is worth remembering that every time the average investor buys or sells a stock, he is probably paying a 2 percent commission. If he buys one stock and sells another, he has suddenly spent 4 percent of his capital. And if he does this 20 times during the year, he had better be making some good returns on those assets, and there had better be good reasons for all of those trades or the broker will have made more than the investor. Avoid multiple transactions; it can become a very expensive game.

Still another red flag is a broker who says, "Here is a wonderful company, the price is right, and I think you ought to buy it for the long term," and then within a very short period of time, without much change in the price, he calls and says "I think you ought to sell it in order to buy this other stock that looks good." If this type of pattern continues on a regular basis, the broker is playing games.

PENNY STOCKS

Brokers who push penny stocks are to be avoided like the plague. There is an illusion in people's minds about low-priced stocks, and acquiescing to that illusion can hurt. People hear stories about Xerox and how the original cost basis of that stock was 10 cents a share, with some investors making a fortune from it over a period of ten years. Consequently, they look for another 10 cent a share stock.

What they forget, however, is that Xerox *never* sold for 10 cents a share. The stock is where it is today due to splitting of shares over a period of years. It was never a penny stock; nevertheless, people think if they buy a stock that sells for a dollar a share and it goes up one point, they will have doubled their money. Likewise, they contend that if they buy a stock at $20 dollars a share and it goes up one point, they will have made only 5 percent. It is not the number of points that is important; it is the percentage change.

Although normal people would rather double their money than make 5 percent, the chances of a double are much more remote than the chances of making 5 percent. In fact, it is my observation that the higher priced stocks tend to be the cheapest. But, because people tend to want to own large numbers of shares as opposed to value (quantity vs. quality), they tend to skip the $100 per share stock in favor of the $10 or $20 per share stock. Remember, numbers of shares is not as important as the rate of return one makes on his invested capital.

Some years ago, there was a wonderful arbitrage opportunity between the stocks of Christiana Securities and DuPont. Christiana Securities was a holding company that owned mostly DuPont stock. If DuPont was selling for $100 dollars a share, Christiana Securities sold for something like $25,000 dollars a share. But although Christiana Securities always sold at a discount to DuPont, because few wanted to own one share of something that cost $25,000, investors really owned the same thing.   Whether one owns a thousand shares at $10 or 500 shares at $20, the same amount of money is involved.   Yet, I have observed a propensity to undervalue the higher priced securities and overvalue the underpriced securities.

"SQUAWK BOX" BROKERAGE

A visit to the neighborhood national brokerage firm will reveal the head office communicating orders and recommendations through an intercom system called the "squawk box." This centralized system, through which headquarters pitches the "stock of the day" for brokers to sell to customers, can be an asset or a liability depending on how brokers use the advice.   Although the analysts who are featured daily on the squawk box come up with fresh ideas for the brokers to sell to the public, the ideas may not necessarily be applicable to the clients to whom the broker is trying to sell.

There is always the danger of using the box to give a broker ideas which he can then sell to his clients.   It is a matter of judgment as to which clients he chooses to sell the idea.   Herein lies the rub of how a broker might treat his clients.   The broker might think, "Well here's an idea.   Now I'm going to call up my 200 clients and give each of them this idea."

This is the objective side of investing, but *subjectively*, it may not be the thing that each client should do.   Suppose, for example, a research firm said, "We recommend the purchase of Commonwealth Edison and the sale of Con Edison." This is objective advice.   They dislike Con Edison, they favor Commonwealth Edison, and their conclusions may be valid.   Let us also assume that they are correct, that Commonwealth Edison is a better investment. Still, it may not be right for me to sell *my* Con Edison and buy Commonwealth because I may have a substantial capital gain on my Con Edison with the result that selling it would incur a needless tax expense.   Therefore, I will have less money with which to re-invest than the difference between those two securities would indicate.

If the broker called me and said, "You ought to do this," he has overlooked the subjective element of my portfolio. The subjective portion is "What is the result to *me* of this transaction?" This is why one needs a broker who can exercise judgment. Such a broker should call and say the following: "My firm thinks that people who own Con Edison ought to switch to Commonwealth Edison. However, I'm suggesting that you *not* switch because my records show that you paid a very low price for your Con Edison five years ago, it has done very well and it will cost you dearly in taxes. I wanted you to know what my firm is recommending, but I don't think you ought to do it."

My confidence factor in that broker skyrockets. He is letting me know the policy of his company, which I think he should. But he is also telling me that he is thinking about *me*. Therefore, the next time he calls me with a recommendation to buy, I will know that it is probably a very honest recommendation, and he thinks it is to my benefit to heed his advice.

On the other hand, however, the broker in Oshkosh, Wisconsin, may not be as current on what is occurring in the financial world as the fellow in charge of research in New York, and Mr. Oshkosh is receiving ideas from an "expert" in New York. The ideas may not be completely correct, but at least there is somebody on top of what is happening, giving advice for the benefit of that broker to pass on to his client. This is a big plus for the client of the wire house broker. The squawk box can also assist in the process of constructive information flow.

There is no question that people in the brokerage industry: a) try to push their own products; b) probably *do* think they are good products; and c) make more money from their own products than by selling non-proprietary products. There is a built-in prejudice to want to make the most money, but this does not necessarily denote dishonesty. Still, it would be surprising for me to receive a call from a wire service retail broker advising me to buy a no-load mutual fund. With no commission, where is the incentive to sell? Instead, the broker will normally try to sell shares of a mutual fund from which he can make a commission, and he will be steadfast in his belief that he is selling a good product. But if a broker were to call and offer a no-load product, I would consider that broker a person of high integrity.

THE BROKERAGE INDUSTRY—A BRAVE NEW WORLD

The banking industry is becoming much more of a factor in brokerage business, not only on the marketing end but also in the underwriting of securities. Whether this is a positive or negative development is debatable. It will certainly give the brokerage industry more capital and stabilize it considerably. To that extent, it is positive. But from the point of view of protection for the depositors, whether the banks should be involved is quite another story. The brokerage business carries with it substantial risks. Even giants like E.F. Hutton and Drexel are classic case studies in mismanagement and financial falls from grace. And, although it can be a very profitable business, many skeptics remain unconvinced that the banking industry should be involved.

Having said this, it is certain that banks will be involved on a grand scale, namely because most brokerage firms have insufficient capital to shoulder the load that they currently bear. The banking system provides the capital to them so they might as well be a part of the banking industry. This is one reason why the bulk of securities activity in Europe and Japan originates from within the venue of large, well capitalized banks. It is inevitable that a similar evolution will occur in the United States.

chapter 19

the best
money managers
I have known

There are two fantastically successful money managers that I have known and respected: T. Rowe Price and John Templeton. These two gentlemen had entirely different philosophies guiding their investment of money, but they had several things in common. They had long-term vision, they had insight, they had a game plan, they were patient, and they were right.

T. ROWE PRICE

I knew T. Rowe Price quite well, and I respected him immensely. The firm carrying his name is headquartered in Bal-

timore, appropriate as he was a native Baltimorean. I also hail
from Baltimore and during the 1960s it was common for the
two of us to lunch together. Mr. Price was a very quiet, unas-
suming man, not particularly effervescent or outgoing, but exceptionally thoughtful.

His story is quite interesting. While he was in the brokerage business during World War II, he observed that the war
was producing plenty of good technology. In addition to electronic technology, he witnessed some great developments occurring in the health care field as a result of the war. For
example, during the war one of the larger goals was to find
cures for ailments like the flu and pneumonia. A product that
emerged from that quest was penicillin, along with other tan-
gential discoveries.

Price also noticed the great strides occurring in radar technology, which was a precursor to television. When the war
eventually ended, he determined that over the next several
years science would make great strides as a result of domestic
application of the technologies created during WW II, and he
decided that this was the place in which to invest. He forecast
the creation of new products and a greater increase in sales and
profits from new products than old ones. In contrast to investment advisors who, at the end of World War II, focused on
consumer-driven companies, which would meet the pent up
demand from the lack of available consumer goods resulting
from the war (automobiles, etc.), Price concentrated on technology and other growth companies. To some, he is the father of
the term "growth stock," famous for the formation of the T.
Rowe Price growth fund, which was the nucleus of what became a very significant organization.

During the mid-1960s, Mr. Price foresaw that the next
major economic problem would be inflation. It is unclear how
he arrived at that conclusion, but once he did he moved swiftly
to invest his personal funds in inflation offsetting assets. He
left the growth stock arena for inflation resistant investing, and

he plowed money into asset companies and invested in oil, gold, and precious metals companies. It took years for him to realize a big profit, just as the growth stock theory took years to pay off.   But the strategy eventually yielded rewards, and handsome ones at that.

Price had the uncanny ability to forecast future trends eight to ten years before they happened, and he was patient enough to wait for them to occur. It is an intriguing exercise to predict what his visionary outlook would be for the next ten to fifteen years. His bias would most likely be toward something very different from inflation or growth industries; it would probably be along the theme of capital spending or the global rebuilding of the infrastructure, a venture of multi-trillion dollar proportions, and an enormous subject in itself.

JOHN TEMPLETON

John Marks Templeton is a gentleman's gentleman. The son of a self-taught Tennessee country lawyer and cotton ginner, Templeton has become one of the premier money managers of our time. He is a soft spoken, almost condescending man who never utters an ill word of anyone and is the epitome of someone who tries to inflict no pain on anyone. He is also a highly religious person and is one of the major grantors of religious awards in the world. Each year, he bestows a religious award, the Templeton Foundation Prize For Progress in Religion, to the person in the world who he thinks has done the most outstanding job. Commencing in 1972, this award has been accompanied by a monetary sum in excess of the amount of the Nobel Peace Prize.

John Templeton is best known as Principal and Founder of the Templeton Mutual Funds, and is also Chairman of an investment management company which, along with its subsidiaries, manages assets in excess of $18 billion.

John Templeton has the same kind of patience and insight as Price but utilizes an entirely different strategy to investing money. Early on, he observed that there were economic booms and recessions throughout the world and that they occurred at different times and in different parts of the world. Therefore, he decided that the proper investment strategy should be global. At the time, almost 40 years ago, this kind of thinking demonstrated a great deal of prescience.

Templeton also decided that the right thing to do was to play the economic cycles in various parts of the world. If he found one area of the world in an economic decline, he would invest his money there until there was a recovery. He shifted funds to wherever a decline had already occurred, instead of to where economies were strong. The result is that Templeton has consistently outperformed the best money managers in the business, over a staggering period of time. Although the research capability behind him may not be the best in the selection of individual securities, it is *extremely* good on long-term timing of economic cycles throughout the world, and I admire him tremendously for his foresight. As an example, he recognized the Japanese market long before others did; he heavily invested in it, and then pulled much of his money from Japan before that market turned downward in the early 1990s.

He is never completely out of any part of the world, but he does shift his money on a worldwide basis. Recently, I remember asking him where he thought the next major breakthrough might be, and he remarked that China would be his best guess, if and when it became available for investment. Indeed, from a fundamental economic point of view, China has more than any nation in the world. It certainly has a labor force which it could employ if it saw fit. Coupled with this is ample natural resources, a good educational system, and superior institutional facilities, although they are relatively small based on the population. Here is where one could envision a major break-

through. When China solves its political problems, it will certainly emerge as a formidable economic powerhouse.

Such are the thoughts of visionary (and successful) investors.

an addendum

chapter 20

the senior
citizen

Throughout my career I have worked closely with senior citizens in the management of their money. I have discovered that contrary to much of the general advice I dispense, senior citizens have special circumstances to consider when investing their capital.

Whatever the amount of capital a senior citizen has, it is probably all he or she will ever have and, unlike others, the risk of short-term loss of capital or income is profound. Since they have concluded the earned income portion of their lives and are dependent on whatever they have accumulated and whatever has accrued for their benefit, there is neither adequate time nor opportunity for them to recoup from a loss.

A CASE IN POINT

On a recent late-night drive through Chicago, I happened to scan the AM radio dial, eventually honing in on a local station which brought in guest financial planning experts for two hours each week to assist call-in listeners.

A conversation ensued between a 64-year old caller, who was a soon-to-be retiree, and the talk show guest for the week, who was touted as an expert in his field. After exchanging pleasantries, the caller described his background. It turned out that his impending retirement as company executive had caused some concern, as it had forced him to focus on the state of his financial affairs. In rummaging over the many financial statements from brokers, he had come to the frightening conclusion that he had not adequately prepared for the inevitable financial period of retirement. He was heavily invested in fixed-income instruments which, he had determined, would be unable to keep him in good stead after inflation. Therefore, he wanted some recommendations for individual stocks.

Before I could sympathize with the caller, the guest offered his two cents worth to the question of which individual stocks the man should consider. "Well," the guest stated, "I hear from many people like you, who really don't have adequate time to analyze the stocks of companies. You spend most of your time—and rightly so—taking care of your business and making money. My suggestion is that you leave the decision of which stocks to purchase to the experts and buy the shares of a good mutual fund."

To many, this would seem to be sound advice. After all, it makes good sense to let a mutual fund manager, who invests for a living, make these seemingly difficult decisions.

But, in fact, the guest expert has committed several errors, not the least of which is that he evaded the question altogether. The caller wants to know which individual stocks to buy, and the expert provided the "populist" response—"Buy a mutual fund."

However, my real problem surrounds a basic logical fallacy which both the guest and, eventually, the caller committed. The soon-to-be retiree works very hard for a living, earning what most would consider a respectable income. He endures all of those long hours, early mornings, late evenings, and extended weekends in order to bring home all of that money. But I submit that the man should also be willing to devote a few hours each week, or a few minutes each day, to account for the status of all of that money. Just because he works hard to *make* the money does not mean that he should work any less hard to *keep* it. Yet, the guest has suggested that he "hand off" to a mutual fund manager the responsibility of investing for his future.

One of my basic contentions is that money management is not a science. Anyone, with even a modicum of effort, can determine the best and the worst 100 companies in America. Experts, analysts, and financial planners are there to assist in this endeavor. But each person should recognize and accept his responsibility in the matter and do his own homework accordingly. The easy way is not also the best way, and the working man as well as the retiree should take stock of their own situations and specific ways to invest as a result.

PLANNING FOR THE FUTURE

By and large, senior citizens are dependant on relatively fixed sources of income such as retirement benefits and Social Security, and although there is some elasticity in these sources of income, it is limited. Therefore, seniors must rely on accumulated capital to bridge the gap between available fixed income and what they require to live each day comfortably.

The senior citizen is not immune to the ravages of inflation. In fact, one of the single biggest expenses, potentially at least, is health care, and the cost of such care has risen faster than the cost of virtually everything else. Therefore, although I believe older people should be conservative in the management of their money, I do not believe their "heads should be in the sand." They, too, have to allow for inflation.

Investment-wise, there are two ways to accomplish this task. One is, of course, to invest for capital appreciation in the equities markets, and the other is to budget to spend something less than available income, reinvest some for the purpose of higher future income, or a combination of both.

On the budgeting side, there are other important issues senior citizens should consider.

First, they should take a hard look at their assets. Those which do not produce income, those which cost money to hold, and those which they cannot liquidate easily should be avoided or sold. I refer to many things, including insurance policies, homes, and other assets which, if sold, could provide capital which, in turn, could provide income or appreciation.

HOUSING

For many, the home is the most valuable asset they hold. And, yet, houses cost money to maintain in the form of taxes, mortgage, maintenance, insurance, and so on. Even after the children have left the "nest," many seniors live in more home than they need. The single biggest reason for this, of course, is that the home is a way of life, and has been for many years, and leaving it for something else is traumatic.

But the fact remains that the home represents idle capital, producing no income, and without the onus of the home, senior citizens could lead a better life, free not only from financial cares but also from day to day living chores.

Congregate living for retired people has become the fashion. Not only can it be less expensive, but it can answer many of the other problems inherent in aging. Traditionally, younger members of the family used to "take in" the older ones, but such is not the case today. The mobility of all people has separated families, and the propensity of all younger people to work has interfered with the traditional family management activities of many.

I have a close association with a company called Life Care Services Corporation. Headquartered in Des Moines, Iowa, it is the leading developer and manager of life care retirement communities throughout the United States. These communities are not nursing homes, nor are they institutions. They are, in fact, communities in which senior citizens live independently but have available to them, within the communities, virtually all of the important necessities for full, productive living.

Residents typically "buy" their apartments or villas, pay a regular maintenance fee, and receive services such as maintenance, housekeeping, food, and medical care when needed. Although each community operates independently and in a slightly different manner, residents often are able to recoup their investment, or a portion of it if they move elsewhere or leave the community altogether.

I have visited dozens of such communities, and I find the residents happy about life in general. And why not? Financially, they have secured good housing at a predictable cost (albeit usually the maintenance fees fluctuate in line with inflation), their housing is managed by professionals and they can lead life as they wish.

There are two other pluses to such communities. First, they provide "peer companionship." That is, automatically, a senior citizen has access to others with common interests, common outlooks, and common problems. This overcomes one of the inevitable fears of senior citizens, that of social isolation.

Second, and not insignificant, is the availability of on-site medical facilities. Access to health care and related assistance assumes an even higher role of importance as people age and require and demand medical assistance, not strictly for major problems but also for many relatively minor ones.

These communities are not "cheap," but in relation to other housing costs and in relation to services available, they represent good value.

There are many other types of retirement communities, some expensive, some not, some offering medical care, some not, some available on a rental basis, others on an "escheatment" of capital basis, and still others on a "return of capital" basis.

The choice of a place to live is varied and is dependent on the way in which a person wants to live, the financial resources available to him, and, of course, both the location and expertise of the professional managers. Such a choice is usually not made lightly, but it can be a good way for a senior citizen to invest capital and receive, in turn, a predictable way of life.

RETIREMENT FUNDS

In recent years, there has been a growing trend to make vested retirement funds "portable." By this, I mean that retirees can withdraw capital, not just periodic payments. For many retirees, this can be most beneficial for purposes of investment or paying off mortgages or other expensive debt. There are tax consequences to such action which seniors should examine on an individual basis before taking action.

One way that retirement assets can be utilized is through a deposit in a "rollover IRA" (Individual Retirement Account), thereby avoiding taxes until withdrawal.

The IRA, a product of the 1980s, has become very valuable to retirees or to those contemplating retirement. For many, contributions are tax deductible; more important, the earnings of such accounts can accumulate and compound tax free. At age 59 1/2, withdrawals from an IRA can be made without penalty, but are subject, of course, to tax; at age 70 1/2, withdrawals must be made in accordance with tables provided by the IRS.

Those who have retired but are not yet 70 1/2 may want to consider spending some other capital, in recognition of an IRA accumulation, thereby saving something in taxes. Of course, each person's circumstances varies and this type of decision requires substantial self analysis.

USE OF TRUSTS

Many senior citizens find it makes sense to create a revocable deed of trust whereby they act as trustee for themselves and, in addition, provide for a successor trustee in case they are disabled or unable to act. Such trusts also enable seniors to avoid certain probate costs at death, as well as direct how the assets of the trust shall be managed or distributed upon death. This can be a valuable tool, providing continuity of management, but there are a few pitfalls.

First, maintaining good and accurate records of which assets are and are not in the trust is vital on a continuous basis. Second, although such a trust acts like a will, it does not preclude the necessity of establishing a will. Third, many confuse the term "probate costs" with estate taxes. A living trust does not necessarily avoid any estate taxes and can make estate administration complicated if not managed properly.

Fourth, the choice of a trustee or successor trustee is vital to the success of such a strategy. Whether to name a family member, a lawyer, or an independent person such as a money manager or a trust company is a decision which can affect the management of the assets. The best advice on this is not to name anyone who may present a "conflict of interest" problem and, of course, not to name anyone who is incapable or unable to manage such a trust.

It goes without saying that the trustee chosen should be one in which the donor has implicit faith.

DISPOSAL OF ASSETS

It is not within my purview to offer estate planning advice. But, of course, senior citizens do have a problem determining how to leave assets upon death and, as a matter of fact, how to dispose of them even while they are living.

I leave to the accountants, the lawyers, and other professionals the advice on this subject. If dispensed properly, this advice will take into account all of the desires of those disposing of assets by will or otherwise, as well as analysis of assets held, tax and legal implications, and family circumstances.

But, from a strict investment point of view, there are a couple of thoughts worthy of consideration.

First, to the extent that a person may plan to leave assets to charity upon death, seniors should consider bestowing such gifts while living.

After all, they are tax-deductible. If an investor owns an asset which has appreciated in value but which pays little income, that asset might be a prime candidate as a gift to charity, thus establishing both a tax deduction and an elimination of tax on a capital gain. In fact, it is quite possible that the gift of such an asset into a charitable remainder trust or in return for an "annuity" from the charity, can also effect an increase in the donor's income.

Second, senior citizens often help subsidize living costs of their children or grandchildren, and this is a worthy goal. But they often overlook the fact that they receive income, pay a tax on it, and then have money to give to family members. Sometimes it makes sense to give capital, rather than income or, in some cases, to establish a trust for the benefit of a family member, thereby eliminating a tax on the income from whatever assets are placed in trust. While such actions require current legal and tax advice, seniors should consider implementing such a strategy.

Third, many people, in considering their estate planning, complicate matters unnecessarily. Many "tie up" money in trust rather than leave it outright, for instance, and try to be all things to all people forever. My strong advice to most is to leave assets upon death to people rather than in trust unless there are compelling reasons for doing otherwise. There exists among many seniors a desire to "manage money from the grave" by restricting how it can be used. But this thinking can actually work to the detriment of the very people a testator wishes to benefit, as vital flexibility in future money management is hindered.

I have one final thought about money management for seniors. I have discovered that many seniors have been remarkably successful in their life endeavors, but upon retirement they become investment and asset managers, something they may not have been before. Therefore, they should obtain advice. But they should also beware. The financial community knows they are good potential customers, and everyone selling anything—bonds, stocks, insurance, gold, annuities, collectibles, real estate, and so on—considers them fair prey. Beware, Senior Citizens, of those who have all the answers about what you should do with your money. It is yours. Keep control of it.

All you need is a little advice and a lot of common sense, most of which, hopefully, you have garnered throughout life's experiences.

epilogue

a true story

Many years ago I gave a talk at a retirement community about the outlook for the economy and the investment markets. At the end of the talk, and in keeping with my usual custom, I asked for questions, complaints, and comments.

One lady stood and asked, "What do you think of the Babson Investment Advisory Service?" I responded that I knew Mr. Babson very well, was familiar with his newsletter, considered it well written and, by and large, a good resource with insightful advice on how to invest money.

The lady replied, "I know all that. But my son tells me that now that I am 106, I should stop worrying about growth stocks. What do you think?"

Without skipping a beat, I responded, "Frankly, I think that if you are 106, you can think about anything you want."

I learned that a year later, at the age of 107, the lady developed a lump in her stomach. The doctor advised against operating because it might be too dangerous. Her reply was,

"Young man, I have no intention of leading life with a lump. Take it out!" He did, and she recovered.

Then, three months later she fell and broke her hip. The doctor told her she would never walk again. She responded, "Young man, I have no intention of living without walking. Fix it." He did, and she walked.

Such is the indomitable spirit of a growth stock investor.

index

227